Olga Bukin, Ilia Bukin, Maxim Bukin

A Complete Guide To Nail

Art

And

Decorative

Manicure

D1465163

Moscow, Russia, 2006

Preface

If you're considering a makeover -- which is always a welcome experience but does take some guts -- then this book is for you. Contrary to the old adage, clothes alone do not make the person. Nice-looking nails count, too.

Every creative individual with good taste and some imagination can potentially turn their nails into a work of art. There're hundreds of thousands of creative people around, but some of them allow their talents to lie dormant within the depths of their inner self. That's exactly why they need this book. It will inspire, direct and assist them on their way.

We don't aim to limit your incentive with a set of nice-and-easy cookie-cutter recipes. Far from that. We will show you how you can hone your skills all by yourself; we'll point out all the possible pitfalls that await you -- at the end of the day, we will assist your professional development and trigger oh so sweet feelings of personal achievement.

This book has been co-written by two nail art specialists and one journalist -- a combination that has proven to work, at least in our experience. It will take you step by step through several difficulty levels, starting with the *least difficult* -- mind you we're not saying the *easy* level as it's our firm belief that the former is the only way to achieve effective and lasting results. But fear not: our book is crammed full of advice, step-by-step tutorials and complementary information. It's structured as a how-to guide: every section of the book will allow you to come up with a finished, professional-quality result. In fact, you can start reading it from whichever page you choose to open: they all contain tons of useful tips that you'll be able to apply straight away.

The authors don't consider this book the absolute truth; we do view it, however, as one of the many ways to find your own creative path in the domain of nail art.

If you'd like to speak to the authors once you've finished

the book, you're very welcome to contact us at <u>ceo@nogti.com</u>

Sincerely,

Olga Petrova, Denis Bukin, Maxim Bukin

Translated by Irene W. Galaktionova and Neil P. Woodhead
Copyright © 2006-2009 by Olga Petrova, Denis Bukin, Maxim Bukin.
ceo@nogti.com
ISBN 978-1-4092-5603-8

Visit us on the web at <u>www.nogti.com</u> and <u>www.nail-art.info</u>

Contents

CHAPTER V. NAIL ART TUTORIALS

CHAPTER VI. SOME USEFUL INFO ABOUT YOUR NAILS   46

Page # 7

SPECIALIST GLOSSARY

Chapter I. History of Nail Art

Having beautiful hands is more than just sporting smooth, silky skin. Your nails -- groomed and well-shaped -- play a big role in the picture, too. Unhealthy, misshapen and untidy nails can ruin even the best-looking hands. Logically, manicure is here to help you perfect them to oblivion, but we can do far better than follow trends blindly or hastily. Fashion is a fickle mistress, after all.

Just think about it: not so long ago designers kept telling us to make sure our lipstick and nail polish were colour-coordinated, implying that a lady should never wear azure on her eyelids, blood-red on her lips and the green of her choice, on her nails.

Okay, so we went along with the trend. And what happened next? Just a few years later, it turns out the combination of blue, red and green *is* the latest trend! Nails have become bright and different, they're covered with glitter and specially designed patterns -- something few trendsetters would ever have imagined. All this colour-uncoordinated, politically incorrect style riot is what Nail Art is all about.

It would be a mistake to think that the craft of adorning one's nails only developed a few years ago. In fact, it counts its history in hundreds of years -- possibly, millennia. It was in Indochina that Western colonists first saw the local ladies sport some beautiful feathers glued on top of their own nails. These days, similar designs can be spotted at European and American parties and fashion shows. New craftsmen have arrived, capable of spending hours over tiny images to turn one's nails into works of art. A session at one such studio, and your nails could rival some of the most famed canvasses.

Like any craft, nail art has its trends, too. Recently, it's the tendency of painting a pattern over a transparent base. A specialist covers a nail -- one of your own or an extension -- with a layer of transparent polish and continues tracing a design of his or your fancy. Hieroglyphics are especially popular at the moment, as well as exotic flowers, geometrical patterns, and Oriental motives. The idea is to leave a few bits uncovered by the design, thus creating the effect of a glass nail.

Classics' aficionados can go for French manicure. Do you know, by the way, that French manicure has as little to do with France as a French kiss? This type of manicure was first introduced by ORLY in 1976, and this company is based in California, in the neighborhood of Hollywood. A film producer asked ORLY's founder Jeff Pink if he could come up with something neutral, so that his actresses didn't need to have their nails redone every time they had a costume change. So Pink created a healthy and well-groomed look by highlighting the tips of the fingernails with bright white polish.

French manicure works best on moderate-length nails with a blunt or rounded tip. It's still popular because it's natural and complements any style, look or even mood of the person who wears it. If you do want to be trendy, you might try to replace the white tips with golden or silver-colored ones. If you do it on one nail only, it'll add finesse to your French manicure. Red nails with blue or green tips are quite popular today. A combination of white and blue looks really nice, too. Just allow yourself to play around a bit with different colors, and the result will cheer you up even on the dullest of days.

After the success of French manicure, Americans decided to come up with another home-based idea for their ladies. Beverly Hills uses very soft, pastel colors that blend naturally, covering the nail from the root to the edge without any sharp contrasts in color.

Later, the so-called American manicure came about. It's best suited for daring and independent ladies. True American manicure calls for bright colors, loud even, on very long rounded nails. This particular style first started to dictate complete color coordination between nail polish and lipstick.

Today though, stylists and designers tend to think you should match your polish to the tone of your eyeshadow. And as the back-to-the-1970s trend is in full swing at the moment, they suggest to keep your polish in the bright pinky, purply lilacky range.

Then there's the Spanish school of manicure that teaches you to seal the base coat with a milky-white layer, to make the following bright-colored coat even more pronounced.

Today, professionals offer nail piercing, as well. If you have the annoying habit of driving everybody mad with studs and earrings in the most unexpected parts of your anatomy, you might want to try it. It's trendy and cool, but unlike pierced lips, noses and such, it doesn't hurt one bit. Also, your nails are one of the few places that can still look elegant, and not just eccentric, when pierced. Double or triple piercings may create some interestingly nice effects there.

Fake nails are best suited for piercings, but if you're not into them, your own will do the trick just as well. You can even adorn them with some jewelry. If you're using fake nails, you can drill a tiny hole in one of them and use it to attach a minute gold or silver pendant. Flat bits of jewelry can be simply glued to the nail with a special solution.

Already thousands of years ago people noticed that the shape of your nails can tell a thing or two about your character and the state of your health. Long angular nails reveal their owners to be realistic and extremely active. They might want to neutralize their excessive energy with some yoga exercises and relaxation techniques. Short square nails point at a reserved and disciplined person, orderly and in control. Oval and conic nail tips often belong to artistic individuals, but also to highly adaptable people, conformists even. Claw-shaped nails may betray an impatient, irritable character, sometimes selfish or even mercenary. Hollow nails may serve as an early sign of neurasthenia.

It goes without saying that polished nails are an important finishing touch to today's women's look. Spoiled for choice, they can spend hours a week over different shades and textures. But do you know that very soon we might be able to change our nails' color in a matter of seconds? You won't even have to remove the old polish and apply a new one. Carlos Gonzalez, a Spanish inventor for the CIDETEC institute, has developed unique fake nails that you can "repaint" by simply sending a command from a special control device.

The technology behind such a breakthrough cosmetic accessory is based on using superimposed layers of electrochromic polymers, electrolytes, and ion-storing polymers that "seal" the resulting hue. To change the color – say, from green to red – all you need is to attach the electrodes and push the button.

Also, the control device is equipped with a tiny preview screen and a scan-like gadget that allows the user to "lift" a particular color from a certain surface, a fabric sample or a magazine page. Mr Gonzalez's invention is already patented and in all probability will find a much wider application than just changing fake nails' color.

Chapter II. Types Of Modern Nail Art

Do yourself a favor one day and put yourself into a professional nail artist's hands. Alternatively, you might want to try your hand at it yourself, in the comfort of your own home. Just spend some time first studying the numerous styles and trends so that the resulting work is not just stupendously pretty but also appropriate.

For instance, stilettos are always popular. But can you wear them with square blunt nails that have recently been just the thing to go with similarly square, blunt heels? Another example: after a considerable lapse, pointy feline nails are back. Which colour complements their shape the most? -- Red, of course! The *femme fatale* look is back with a vengeance and is no longer considered vulgar. The adolescent waif, however, has become rather *passé*.

Besides red, orange and fuchsia are also in vogue at the moment. Five or so years ago, a colour combination like this would have scandalised anyone. Now, it's the hottest thing around. And as for business ladies, the latest trend is to adorn their nails with company logos.

Another idea for today's nail art is to replicate your clothes' fabric pattern, designs varying from polka dots and herringbones to animal prints. Real fabrics have their use in nail art, too, especially lace, ribbon lace and nets.

Chapter III. Tools And Materials

Nail Polish

Chemical Composition

Most of the time, all we remember is that nail polish is a viscous chemical substance whose chief property is its color. The nail polish spectrum is similar to lipsticks in its abundance of shades -- it's bigger, even, because it includes the cool colors which are absent from lipsticks. Some manufacturers offer their customers dozens, even hundreds of different shades.

So let's see now what goes into our nail polish because every ingredient adds something to its practical value.

The main component of all nail polish is nitrocellulose. This substance is responsible for film forming and the adherence properties of your polish. If it's not diluted to the necessary consistency with other ingredients, your whole artwork will just peel off your nail.

Another ingredient is a challenge to spell: toluene sulfanilamide formaldehyde resin. Its main task is to ensure quality shine after the polish has dried out, but it improves its adherence, too.

Today's nail polish also includes the so-called plastisizers. Usually they're castor and camphor oils, as well as butyl stearate. They improve flexibility of your polish so that it covers your nail without clumping. Other resins are used in polish, too: they improve its shine and adherence, and serve as a filler.

Solvents are also used in nail polish, such as acetone, petroleum ether, butyl and ethyl acetate. They help to thin polish down to the desired concentration and are also responsible for its drying-out times. Color pigments can be obtained from iron and titanium oxides: they are called coloring agents and are responsible for the basic color of your polish. Tiny quantities of organic pigments, like micas for pearly polishes, may also be added.

Another excellent, highly useful ingredient is an ultraviolet stabilizer. Its task is to prevent fading when your nails are exposed to sunlight. And finally, nutritional agents like calcium and keratin or other proteins whose responsibility is nail-strengthening and moisturizing. But do make sure you read the label before buying: you might find some of the above missing from certain polishes.

Consumer Properties

Good polish is as precious as a piece of jewelry. Just imagine that this tiny little pot contains a magic liquid whose color (provided it's applied correctly) can immediately cheer you up and inspire your friends' admiration. Ain't it a jewel? Good polish isn't supposed to dry out half a year after you've bought it, either. Expiry dates for polishes do exist though, which are usually about a year and a half after purchase or production. The more time has passed since its purchase, the drier your polish gets, but this problem can be solved with the help of ordinary solvents. It's better to try thinning your polish when it's slightly thick, not when it's entirely dry.

Sometimes you can see special polish thinners, but most people do it with ordinary nail polish remover. Pay attention though that your polish remover doesn't contain any potentially polish-harming additives, like oils, perfume or various nutritives. You can't expect miracles: once you've thinned your polish a couple of times, it'll be ruined anyway, as it'll develop all sorts of clots, bubbles, and won't cover the nail properly.

It might sound too simple, but the only way of telling good polish from bad is by trying it. Still, let's discuss a few major points that might help you make the right choice.

First, pay attention to the color. Try to visualize the polish on your nails -- sometimes it's enough to realize it won't suit you.

Remember that testing it on white paper won't give you a realistic idea of what the polish is going to look like on your nails. The only thing tests are good for is to assess the polish's transparency -- that is, how many coats you'll need. Remember that polishes in cool shades suit warm-colored hands, and vice versa.

Second, assess the polish's transparency. If it's too transparent, it would be better to apply it over a thicker polish that would serve as a base (a white background, for instance). You can only judge the color adequately by seeing it on finished nail samples.

Third, you need to open the pot and assess the polish's consistency. Lift the brush to see how long it will take for the drop on its tip to fall. It must happen within five seconds, otherwise it means the polish is too thick, won't adhere to the nails properly and will dry out soon.

Fourth, have a close look at it. The brush should have even, smooth and springy hairs and should be rather longish, about 1.5 centimeters. Scrutinize the pot itself: if the label is glued sideways, if the lettering has rubbed off, if the bottle is scratched and deformed, it's best not to buy it because in this case, most likely the outside reflects the inside. It's better to buy polish that contains special metallic mixing balls on the bottom. When you shake the bottle, you'll easily achieve a uniform, smooth mixture.

Manufacturers And Prices

Every country's market is unique. Sometimes you come across a totally unknown company that produces outstanding polishes, true wonders of chemical engineering. But you can never be sure, so it's best not to take risks and trust the time-tested suppliers who guarantee the uniform quality of their merchandise every time.

We've come up with the following classification of nail polish manufacturers:

- **Exclusive professional brands.** Expensive and not easy to lay your hands on. Polishes that cost $30-50 and more for a bottle never reach shop counters: they're used in the film industry, and also by top makeup artists and models shooting covers for leading glossies. You won't find them in your favorite shop round the corner: polishes like these can only be bought in specialized boutiques.
- **Professional brands.** These are names like LCN, Akzent Direct, Creative Nail Design or OPI. Some manufacturers, like ORLY, offer two types of products, targeting both professional and consumer markets. They're usually priced at $6 to $20, the average price being about $7.
- **Consumer brands.** That's what you buy in cosmetics and drug stores -- Revlon, Paloma, Lakme, Bourjois, Margaret Astor, Maybelline, Green Mama, to name just a few. They're priced at $3 to $10, the average being $5.
- **Budget brands.** That's the stuff you see at street markets and in dollar stores. Some of them are legitimate manufacturers targeting the budget consumer, like Golden Rose, Veronique, Catherine Arley or Gala. Others produce bootleg copies of famous makes. Sometimes you can't even tell the manufacturer at all! Prices vary from $0.7 to $2, the average being $1.

Each manufacturer has their own strong and weak points. But once you've shopped for polish a few times, you'll learn to differentiate and choose the make that works for you. It's no brain surgery, really. Professional products do differ from consumer ones in their quality, but not too dramatically. You may even come across a consumer make that's better than a professional one: so good luck, your experience will be your best teacher.

One thing that differenciates between professional and consumer makes is that their products may contain certain very specific additives. Professional-brand polishes have very strict contents standards. Budget makes can deviate from the standard in most unexpected ways, so you can never tell what you're buying.

Types of Polish

You can't even start to imagine the amount of amazing nail care substances out there. Let's begin with defining their main types.

- **Base coat.** It protects your nails from the following layer of colored polish as well as improves its adherence properties. Can vary greatly: from plain colorless polish and treatment coats to strengthening formulas, etc. – basically, everything that serves as a first layer is called a base coat (it also includes ridge fillers).
- **Top coat** serves to cover the finished nail in order to protect it from scratches and enhance the color. It's either plain transparent polish or special-purpose transparent top coats: speed-dry, high-gloss or matt-finish. This is what you conclude your work with, to seal the result.
- **Main coat.** Usually it's colored polish. It's sandwiched between the base and top coats and provides the color we've chosen to wear. The main coat can be of any color at all.

Apart from these, there're zillions of various polishes available today, not to forget treatment and strengthening formulas. Don't feel too intimidated by this abundance: they all serve their purpose. Let's try to classify their functions:

- **Treatment polishes.** They gradually improve the state of your nails so they must be used regularly. Just make sure you understand that although their primary purpose is healing, they're not exactly prescription or even over-the-counter medications. Their results are rather vague and may vary considerably in different users. If you do decide to try them, you'll need to closely monitor the state of your nails during the treatment period. Please remember that calcium-containing formulas should not be used for too long or too often. Oil products soften the cuticle; vitamin-containing ones enhance growth. Please remember they're only good in moderation, and during the course of treatment it's advisable to stick to plain no-frills manicure.

- **Strengthening polishes.** These contain acrylic, silk, vinyl or other such substances. They don't treat your nails but they offer better protection and strength as long as you wear them. They can serve as a base coat, especially for nail art work.
- **Special-purpose top coats:** fast-drying, glitter, etc.

If you're familiar with types and properties of different nail polishes, you can choose the ones you need.

Type Of Polish	Properties	Purpose & Application
Regular Color Polish **Figure # 01**	The most common and popular type.	You'll need two coats of it, with the exception of black and very dark polishes that require only one, and white or very pale ones that need three coats for each nail.
Pearly Polish	Has a typical pearly sheen and lasts well.	Has a visible texture so make sure you apply it in one direct stroke from the nail base right to the tip.

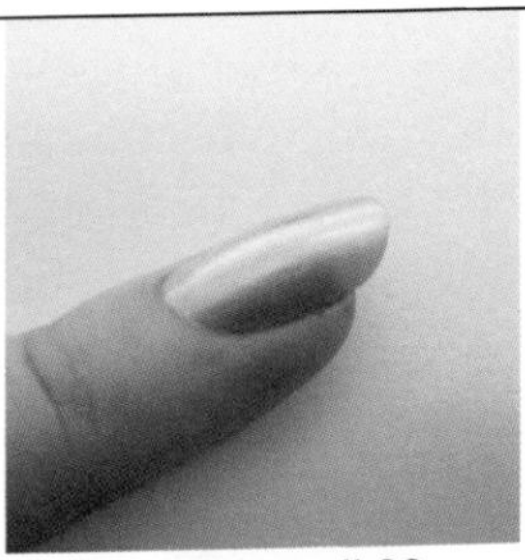

Figure # 02

Transparent Polish	Can be used as a base or top coat. Serves to protect and enhance the color and shine of your polish. Contains aniline colors. Protects nails from staining.	
Base Coat	Serves as primer, to level out the nail's surface. Can be pink or transparent.	Basically,it's transparent polish specially formulated to be used as a base. Usually contains nail treatment ingredients.
Fast-drying	Express drying times, touch-dry in about a minute.	Usually it's for top coats, but some color polishes can be fast-dry, as well.
Glitter Polish	Transparent or color polish containing bits of glitter in various shapes, shades and sizes.	There's a risk of scratching your nail with them when removing glitter polish, so make sure you use it over a special base or a layer of transparent polish.

 Figure # 03		
Matt And Frosty Polishes Figure # 04	They don't offer the smooth sheen other polishes have. Their surface is smooth and velvety. Thick, they dry out in no time.	Their clear varieties, usually targeting male consumers, add matt finish to any color underneath. Unfortunately, they wear out quickly leaving exposed patches of glossy surface underneath.
One-Coat Polish	Thick and viscous.	One layer is enough for each nail. It does wear out and peel very quickly, though.
Strengthening Polish	Contains silk fibers and keratin. Protects the nails from environmental exposure. It's basically a top coat with special additives.	Applied at the end of your manicure session, it serves to harden the nails.
Bitter Polish	Clear or green-tinted.	Tastes bitter and serves as a deterrent, helping to kick the nail-biting habit.
Hypoallergenic Polish	Usually available in	Contains no

	pharmacies, it comes with nickel-free mixing balls.	contact allergens, no sulfanilamide formaldehyde resins, and is toluene-free.
Mood-Changing Polishes	Their colors change their hues at different angles.	
Heat-Sensitive Polishes **Figure # 05**	They gradually change their color as they react to the nail surface temperature that in turn depends on body heat or outdoor conditions.	As the tip of the nail is usually colder than its base, it results in a subtle French manicure effect.
Crackle Polish	The look is reminiscent of antique crackle finish.	Three seconds after application it starts to shrink, creating a thin gossamer of tiny cracks.
Watercolor Polish	Transparent polish in different shades. It's shinier than conventional ones, as if it's not completely dry yet. The resulting color is soft and gentle.	Works well with French manicures smoothing out the sharp color border between the nail base and the tip. Its transparency offers itself to nail art, adding depth to your design.
UV-Sensitive Polish	It changes its color to bright pinks, blues, reds, turquoises or greens when exposed to a source of UV	

	light in a disco, bowling alley or nightclub, or in a casino.	
Creamy Polish	Contains thick insoluble pigments. May go stripey when applied which can in turn create some interesting nail art effects.	
Mica-Based Polish **Figure # 06**	A bit rough to touch, it contains large mica pigments.	
Peel-off Polish	Water-based, it contains some specific polymers. Not suitable for pedicure.	Can be removed in a single piece.
Nail Art Paints	Richer in color and thinner in texture than regular polishes.	Professional nail art paint kits usually contain six bottles of different colors: e.g., red, blue, black, white, yellow, and green. This type of polish is more uniform, and colors are more pronounced. Can be used in nail art

		like traditional paints. Each bottle contains a special brush for painting stripes. It works especially well over an unconventional base: pearly, mood-changing, etc. Available in professional salons, specialized shops or online, by a bottle or in a kit. Special brushes are recommended for better results, sold separately.
Mini Nail Polishes	Containing only about 3.5 ml, they can fit into a smallest makeup bag. The brush reaches the bottom of the bottle, so a mini polish stays fresh longer and gets used up completely.	
Collection Polishes	Their release is timed to coincide with a new season (as in winter, spring, summer, or fall collections), event, or location (a nightclub). Can be put together by type (watercolor), properties (hypoallergenic),	

	purpose (e.g., for soft nails) and so forth. They tend to be discontinued just as you've acquired a taste for them! Seasonal collections aim to mirror the ideas of the season they target. They make part of a current look and help in creating it.	

The Rhinestone Magic

Figure # 07

Rhinestones are minute crystals or gem imitations made of glass, crystal, plastic, lightweight metal, etc. You arrange them on your nails to create designs that are pretty and unique: they're so small and difficult to lay every nail will end up looking different from the rest.

They come in many colors, shapes and sizes (usually 1 to 3 mm in diameter). Can be sold by the piece, in 10-piece sets and in pots containing 80 to 100 rhinestones. Many nail art designs include them as decorative elements.

Please note that at the moment, the market is flooded with cheap plastic rhinestones of dubious quality. They offer a great variety of shapes but after applying a top coat, they turn dull. They may also have deformations, sharp scratchy edges, etc.

Application. Apply a dot of special glue or transparent polish to the nail. Using a wet toothpick or needle, pick up a rhinestone, place it over the dab of glue and press very lightly. Finish off with a layer of transparent polish or a top coat.

Micro Glitters And Glitter Dust Powder

Figure # 08

We all know the type of glitter used in makeup: it makes one's skin look amazing, creating some incredible effects depending on the lighting. It does the same for your nails so it's often used to create party nail art designs. It's basically the same glitter as in glitter polishes, only in powder form. But the beauty of it is, you have control over its quantities.

Application. Apply a layer of transparent polish and sprinkle some glitter over it. After it's dry, brush the extra ones off using a soft brush. You can use a palette for this purpose, too: just apply a drop of transparent polish onto a palette, add the desired quantity of glitter and mix it in, then use the resulting mix on your nail.

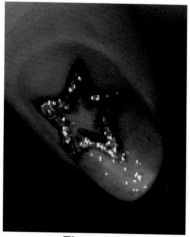

Figure # 09

You can also use glitter to create original mirror effects. To do this you'll need some really good quality homogenous tiny circle or square-shaped glitter, but not strips or powder. When shopping for your glitter, press it to the side of the plastic bag it comes in for a quick check on its smoothness and shine: its appearance is what you'll later get on your own nails.

After that, it's easy:

- Prepare the nail in covering it with a layer of transparent polish and wait until it's completely dry;
- Apply a second coat to two or three nails at a time and wait until it's touch-dry – that is, when it doesn't stick to your fingers any more but still feels slightly soft to the touch;
- Sprinkle a generous thimbleful of glitter onto a sheet of paper, dip your finger in it and press your nail into the glitter as if to rub it in;
- Shake off any extra glitter. You'll end up with a shiny, mirror-like surface.
- Apply a transparent top coat.

Foil

This thin metal film can also be used in nail art, especially considering all its various types.

Type Of Foil	Properties	Purpose & Application
Metallic Wrap	Comes in special packs in various colors and shapes.	Apply it over transparent polish or specially-formulated adhesive and smoothen out with a little stick. If desired, can be finished with a layer of transparent polish which will improve its durability but reduce its depth and shine.
Transfer Foil	Attached to the nail with special adhesive, it can differ greatly in its colors and patterns.	Apply some adhesive to the desired part of the nail, press some foil to it (face side down), hold for a while, then remove the foil's base layer.
Smooth Foil	Regular foil used in chocolate wrappers.	Can be cut into all sorts of different bits, strips and

		shapes. You can then place them over a thick, springy piece of rubber to punch tiny patterns in them with special little drills sharpened at different angles. You then lay them out on your nail to create desired shapes. Tiny foil and plastic shapes are also available in various colors, like little hearts, stars and such. Furthermore, you can roll bits of foil into tiny little balls to serve as flower hearts in your designs.
Foil Strips 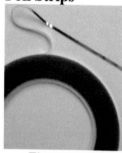 **Figure # 10**	Gold or silver, they can come with their own adhesive base. You can make them yourself, too, using plain smooth foil. They are also available as gold and silver leaf: it's used over specially-formulated adhesive and finished off with a top coat.	Adhesive-base strips are applied over dry polish. The smooth-foil self-made ones, over transparent polish or adhesive. You can use strips to make tiny snake designs by folding them, bit by bit, at 90 degrees while changing directions. Folding strips at other angles can give you lots of various shapes you can then use in your designs.

Nail Art Jewelry

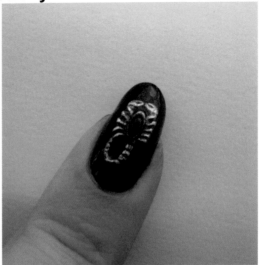

Figure # 11

A bindi is a small piece of jewelry suitable for nail art. They're flat shapes made of precious metals—or, more particularly, of gold, because nobody seems to produce silver bindis suitable for nail art. It's a shame really because not all of us are into gold. Then again, the choice of gold bindis is quite limited, too: most of the time it's standard sticker-kit heart shapes, cute little angels, tiny umbrellas and such.

And still. If you can't see yourself wearing gold, go to a jeweler's and get yourself a cheap pair of studded silver earrings, no more than 5 millimeters thick. Use a pair of pliers to cut the stud off, then file the remaining bump down with a diamond file (the first stage of the process takes 2 to 3 minutes including the preparatory fumbling, the second, about five, just make sure the resulting piece stays, well, in one piece). The newborn silver bindi can then be used in the same way as gold ones.

Their use is simple: just glue them onto a nail with some adhesive or transparent polish, then cover with several layers of top coat or transparent polish. The best way is to use them on the same fingernail (e.g., on the middle finger) on both hands. The other nails are then covered with matching abstract designs, otherwise it all gets too busy.

Some other nail art jewelry includes rings, studs and pendants, sometimes with tiny gemstones. They can serve as piercing accessories and sometimes look identical to bindi shapes.

A gold nail is yet another accessory. You glue it on top of your own as you would a fake nail, the only difference being you can't file a gold nail! Usually it also has a gold chain ending in a ring, which serves as a separate decoration and ensures you don't lose the precious nail (they start at $20). If you can't find them in a shop, you might try to have them made to order, as long as you can clearly explain your idea to the jeweler. Give him exact measurements and decide on the future item's weight and caratage: the jeweler's charges will depend on them.

Tattoos

Figure # 12

Yes, exactly. Just don't get scared, because tattoos can be a great nail art accessory. They can even become a centerpiece of a stunning design, as long as they're approached responsibly and professionally.

When working on a brand-new design, consider the fact that a tattooed wrist can add to it in a most unexpectedly charming way. You don't have to have a permanent tattoo – which is more, you shouldn't have it because the skin on your wrist is extremely thin and vulnerable, making a tattoo potentially dangerous. A temporary tattoo is a much nicer idea.

A permanent tattoo is a type of surgery when a specialist uses a thin, short needle to insert specially-formulated ink into the top layers of your skin. One prick of the needle results in one tiny dot in the design; the tattoo machine works very quickly though so all you feel is a burn. The design can be in any colors you like, but remember that light colors are almost unseen on fair skin, and vice versa.

Overall, tattooing is an art so make sure you find a good, responsible professional, even if it costs you much more. Decide on the pattern you choose to wear, and bring a sketch of it along. Ask the tattooist to draw the exact design on a sheet of paper: improvisation has no place in his line of work.

It takes a finished tattoo about a week to heal. During that time it's covered with a scab, like any other wound. You should never pick it. When the scab falls off, it'll reveal your tattoo underneath, but the colors won't look as bright as they did right after the surgery.

Temporary tattoos use natural dyes instead of ink. They wear out quickly and the design will disappear accpordingly. Easy! Here's the method:

- Make sure your skin is oil- and lotion-free by applying some rubbing alcohol or nail polish remover;

- If the henna pack doesn't contain it, rub some Eucalyptus oil in;
- Create a desired design by squeezing some henna mix out of the cone onto your skin, with or without a stencil. The thicker the henna layer, the brighter the resulting color, so it should be 2 to 3 millimeters thick.
- As the henna mix dries out, apply some lemon juice to the pattern every 30 minutes or so. After the henna mix has stayed on the skin for two hours, remove and discard it but don't attempt to wash the pattern for another 24 hours.
- At first your tattoo will appear to be light brown but it'll get darker after 24 hours.

You can make your own henna mix:

- Make some very strong tea (the stronger the tea, the darker the resulting tattoo);
- Mix half a cup of the tea with juice of half a lemon and two tablespoonfuls of castor sugar;
- Use this brew to mix with henna powder to make a thick paste;
- Let set for another 15 minutes;
- Place the mix into a cone or a paint tube. Will keep in the fridge for a couple of days.

It's even easier to make a temporary tattoo with some water-resistant felt tip pens, available in craft shops. First, rub some nail polish remover into the skin to make it oil-free. Then, draw a design on it using water-resistant felt tip pens. It'll last one or two days which will do for a night out. In the absence of water-resistant felt tip pens, a regular gel pen or acrylic paints will do the trick nicely, but the design will wash off your hands during the first restroom trip.

Special stickers are also available, aimed to imitate tattoos: a ready-made transparent-base design is stuck onto your skin. They don't last, but are equally quick to apply.

The main "survival trick" to remember is that any tattoo can be used to complement a nail art design which can repeat the tattoo's pattern symmetrically or only use one or two elements of it. Just don't go over the top: everything looks great in moderation.

Other Accessories

There're too many to even start; so we'll stop in some detail on the main ones that you might want to consider when working on your personal look. Please mind that this list of accessories and their properties is far from extensive: every specialist might add to it his or her own ideas and discoveries that make them and their customers stand out in the city crowd!

Type Of Accessory	Properties	Purpose & Application
Colored Ribbons	Adhesive-based ribbons come in many colors and patterns, e.g. "snake skin", 2 to 3 mm thick	Are glued on top of dry polish. It's important to remember, when applying them, to make sure their ends don't touch the skin and don't surpass the edges of the nail.
Lace	It's finer than regular lace, and comes in various colors and patterns. One of the most common ones is a simple fine net.	Can be used as cut-out fragments or as a whole piece and is glued to the nail with adhesive or transparent polish
Stickers	They differ in design and application modes.	Their application may differ. Self-adhesive

 **Figure # 13**	Designs are countless but they don't boast much variety, boiling down to cute heart shapes, little flowers and leaves. You'll be hard pressed to find a sticker featuring a death's head or a cute little coffin. Despite all their multitude, stickers can't outdo an exclusive designer job. They're good when you're pressed for time and have to come up with something decent pretty quickly. Some stickers can be very pretty and contribute to a lovely work of nail art if used correctly. Some of them are like gold and silver fish scales; others contain rhinestones and bits of glitter. Yet others are little pictures, while the fourth are lengths of imitation leather, fabric or net that can be cut to fit certain parts of your designs.	ones are removed from their base and stuck onto the nail. Others have to be moistened with water first, then left for a few minutes. After that you peel them off onto your finger, face down, attach to the nail, then hold for a while.
Feathers	They're not used too often as understandably they're awkward to wear. They usually make part of evening and special-occasion designs. You can buy	Attach one or two feathers to a nail using special adhesive or transparent polish so that the bulk of the feather stretches beyond the tip of the

	special nail art feathers, big or medium-sized, imitating those of exotic birds. You can also use plain feathers available from souvenir shops. You can always pull a couple out of a pillow or borrow from a chicken. Any hard and smallish feathers will do, like those of parrots, nightingales, quails or guinea fowl.	nail. It's best to limit it to one nail only, covering the others with similarly-styled small patterns. Another good idea would be to use the feather as an imaginary bird's tail, and paint the birdie on the nail itself.
Colored Bullions  Figure # 14 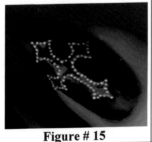 Figure # 15	Tiny round-shaped grains of pearly, silver, and golden colors, sometimes also blue and green.	Dip a thin brush (or a needle, or a toothpick) into a wet sponge, and use it to fish a few grains out of the pot. Then you place them onto a nail over some adhesive or transparent polish. You'll need two or three layers of top coat to fix them safely in place: because of their shape and size, bullions are vulnerable to abuse and their top layer comes off very easily.
Dried Flowers and Plants	You can use dried seeds and flowers in nail art, as well as other parts of a plant. Poppy seeds are good, but	Tiny dried flower petals work well. You might check crafts and gift shops for already-dried and painted

	don't forget the humble straw we all remember from school crafts lessons, used to create collages on pieces of paper.	flowers, ready for use. For instance, tiny sprigs of dill, dried and painted, would look truly original in a rhinestone design. Seeds—dyed or natural-colored—are glued onto a nail to form little flowers or as part of an abstract design. Flat seeds are especially good for this purpose, like those of bell peppers, dill, or lady's purse.
Threads	Available in nail art shops and salons. They are made of different materials and differ in color and twining. Ordinary threads for gold and silver embroidery can be used in nail artwork, too.	The most important thing to remember when glueing them to a nail is to make sure the length of thread doesn't touch the cuticle on one side and doesn't quite reach the tip of the nail on the other. Then it's covered with a top coat or some transparent polish. You can lay them out in lines or use them to create shapes like nets, or you can roll small lengths into rings or fold and glue them to shape triangles, squares, etc.
Correction Pen	Used to remove little mistakes, it has an internal chamber filled with polish remover.	A tiny piece of cloth soaked with polish remover will work just as well.

Polish Remover	Most importantly, do not buy acetone-based removers. Acetone has a drying effect and using it will result in fragile nails that break easily.	
Acrylics and Gels	At first, their use was limited to nail extensions until the nail art adopted the new techniques to its own shape-creating purposes. Acrylic is a thick self-hardening substance used to shape various 3-D nail design details. Gels harden when exposed to UV rays. They are thinner than acrylic therefore harder to shape but good for creating flat patterns that can then be attached at any angle to the nail.	

Nail Art Tools

It's impossible to create a fine work of art without properly chosen tools: they are the instruments of turning several meaningless details into a finished design. Interestingly, you won't find anything new here: you're already familiar with all the tools used in nail art practice. Choosing and using them though is another thing altogether.

Needles And Toothpicks

These two serve two purposes. Keep in mind that needles tend to prick, so yours must be clean -- by no means rusty! -- and acquired from trusted sources. Best of all, just buy it as part of an ordinary sewing kit.

Disinfect your needle often with some rubbing alcohol and use with extreme care: it's all too easy to hurt your own hands with it. The best needle, from a nail artist's point of view, is rather thin and of medium length (although of course the user is the best judge). It has to be easy to grip quickly so that it doesn't slide out of your fingers in a hurry.

Toothpicks are easy: they break often so the best thing would be to buy a big pot of them at once, you'll need it. They should preferably be rather sharp and, like needles, of medium length. Both can be replaced by a thin, short brush.

In nail art, these tools are mainly used to create the so-called marble effect. It's very easily done: paint a nail with a color of your choice (it's best to keep it neutral, like white, black or transparent). Make sure you apply it in a nice thick layer, as long as the polish doesn't leak or cake in a nasty clot on the tip. Straight after that, place a couple of dots of a different-color polish (a contrasting color would work best) -- even several colors, if desired. Swirl them all together with a needle or toothpick, let dry and finish with a layer of transparent polish.

A bit of advice: it's a good idea to choose related colors, and especially to add some glitter in a similar shade. For instance:

- blue, sky-blue, silver (black, white)
- red, pink, silver
- yellow, green
- yellow, blue
- lilac, blue

When swirling it together, make sure you do it in a particular style: e.g., keep going in one direction only, or zigzagging, or in spirals, nets, in parallel or vertical strokes. The funny thing is, no matter how hard you try, every nail will end up looking different from the rest, making it the strongest and the weakest point of this method.

Gel Pen

An ordinary gel pen used in schools, offices and at workplaces can prove truly universal in creating all sorts of designs for your little nails.

Its fortes are obvious: the resulting line is sharp, thin and even, which allows for a clear, easy to remove pattern. It has weaknesses too, though, like a limited color scheme. Also, it's tricky to use on your own right (or left, if you're a leftie) hand. But once you know what you're doing, these problems can be overcome.

Here's some basic advice on how to create a nail art design with the help of a gel pen:
- apply two coats of polish. The polish should be touch-dry: it shouldn't stick to your hands, nor should it be soft, but it mustn't be completely dry, either;
- use a gel pen to draw a pattern on your nail as you would on paper. At first, you might find it hard to make the pen write, but it will in the end if you retrace every line a few times;
- if you're creating a complex design, it's best to limit it to one nail only, and do the rest with some elements of the major design;
- as a finishing touch, seal the design with a coat of transparent polish, but only after the picture has completely dried out. This especially applies to metallic-colored gel pens.

Brushes

Almost everyone who has ever visited an arts class knows what brushes are. Nail art uses them mainly to add fine detail to a completed design. Knowing how to paint with brushes renders you more professional than limiting yourself to an ordinary gel pen: specialists appreciate a natural stroke.

Of course, it takes a bit of time to master nail art brushes, but in the end, it comes. At first, it's best to use fake nails and special practice hands. Nail art brushes vary greatly in their shape and size.

Type Of Brush	Purpose & Properties
Dotting Tool	Instead of bristles, it ends in a tiny pellet, like a ballpoint pen. It can be used to create dots and tails by dipping the tip of the dotting tool into polish. The resulting little blob, while not quite dry yet, can be then flattened or smeared out.
Fan Brush	It does look like a fan. Drop two or three blobs of different-colored polishes onto a palette and pick them up with the fan brush in one smooth scoop so they don't mix. If you then draw the brush along a nail, you'll get overlapping colored bleed lines. You can use it to paint wavy lines, too, that make an excellent background for nail art designs.
Striper	It's long -- 20 to 30 millimeters -- and about 1 to 2 millimeters thin. Is excellent for drawing straight and curvy lines. Held vertically upright, a short one is used for painting swirls.
Shading Brush	About 4 millimeters wide, it's good for painting multicolored patterns when you pick up two or three different colors

	onto the brush at the same time.
Dagger Shading Brush	Same as a shading brush, but one side of it is cut at an angle. Perfect for painting little leaves, flower petals, etc.
Round Brush	Fat with a sharp tip, it's great for color-filling and applying glitter.
Detailer, Medium Figure # 15	About 5 to 8 millimeters long and 1 to 2 millimeters thick, it's the most widely used nail art working tool. Use it to paint swirls, middle-thickness lines, dots, etc.
Detailer, Fine	2 to 4 millimeters long and 0.5 to 1 millimeter thick. You only need it to paint very fine details. It's hard to work with, so using it requires a lot of practice.

Piercing

Some people's passion for having the most unexpected parts of their bodies pierced, including the most intimate ones, has finally reached the nails, too. There's even a suitable motto these days, "It doesn't hurt to have your nails pierced!" Sure it doesn't hurt: the nail plate doesn't contain any nerve endings able to register pain. But it won't be long before the pierced nail starts to break or even crumble, so the first question you need to ask yourself, is, "Am I really sure I need it?"

A piercing is a tiny hole in your skin that holds a piece of jewelry. Professional nail artists make it with a special piercing drill. They place your nail face down onto a special elastic pad and point the drill at the inner side of its tip. Then they drill a hole trying to not press the drill too hard but rather make sure it contacts the nail at all times.

It takes more time to drill through a natural nail than it does through a fake one. They differ in density, as well as shape: real nails tend to be uneven. A hand drill has a key on its other end that serves to screw on stud-based jewelry. An electric drill should be used with extreme care: it drills a hole in no time so it takes all your concentration not to ruin a nail.

If you don't have a drill you might try to pierce a hole yourself with a heated needle. The smell that accompanies this bit of "surgery" is truly obnoxious, but the procedure won't hurt a bit. Take a fat needle, hold it for a few moments over a candle flame and immediately press its end to the inside of a nail tip. Be doubly careful not to burn yourself! It's best you decide first where exactly you want the hole to be, and mark the spot before you start. Here're a few tips to get you going:
- support yourself by placing both your elbows on the table;
- it's better to take your time taking aim than miss in a hurry;
- the burnt nail smell will go away after a couple of minutes;
- do not use your own fingers to support the nail you intend to pierce. Needles have a nasty habit of slipping out of hands, which may result in an unnecessary injury;
- keep the nail you intend to pierce suspended in the air while the elbow is firmly propped on the table;
- do not pierce the tip too close to the nail's edge.

Use the resulting hole to insert all sorts of little pendants, chains and studs. They are available in specialized stores, nail art salons, or online. You can also use ordinary jewelry, like tiny pendants or chain links. Put a chain link through the hole and press the ends together with special pliers or a pair of tweezers. You can also use some pretty threads to put them though the hole: it's a good idea to fluff up their ends and glue them over the nail.

Nail Files

A file is a personal fast-response tool. They can be diamond, sapphire, ruby-based, ceramic or emery boards. Emery boards are mainly used for polishing.

The best file to use is a ceramic two- or three-sided one. The rest, with the exception of sandpaper ones, can ruin the nails. Use the coarser side of the file to shorten and shape the nail, and then the finer side to smoothen out the edges. We suggest you keep a nail file on you at all times.

Files for natural and fake nails differ, too. Those for real nails are softer and less abrasive. The last word in the nail file world is a triple-cut metal file that, unlike diamond ones, doesn't split the nail plate. When you use them, the edge of the nail gets caught between the file's teeth that cut the extra off.

We suggest you buy ceramic files as their abrasive properties guarantee their quality. You should look for those with medium grit: coarse grit is something you need for nail extensions, while fine-grit files are mainly good for polishing. If you're looking for quality, long-lasting files, specialized salons are the places to shop for them. They cost about $10 but will last 3 to 4 years provided you're buying them for personal use. To compare, an ordinary store-bought nail file costs $1 to $5 and might last half a year, after which its abrasive surface will wear out or get clogged up. But of course, it's up to you to decide which file really appeals to and works for you.

Buffer Blocks

A nail buffer block is a contraption that serves to remove oil from the nail's surface or to slightly file it down. Because it removes a nail's upper layers, it's not recommended for frequent use. Have mercy on your poor nails!

A buffer block has an elongated shape and is covered with

a special material similar to soft sandpaper. It's comfortable to hold, and because of its elastic properties, it covers the whole surface of the filed nail. Buffer blocks are used to remove oil from the nail's surface, to even out ridges or scales, or to rub off the cuticle. They're available in specialized professional stores and salons, and cost about $10.

Cuticle Pusher

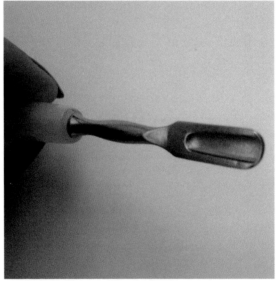

Figure # 16

As its name suggests, it serves to push away the cuticle -- a hard, dry strip of dead skin along your nail base. It should be used with caution: always make sure you've softened the cuticle first, and then proceed with care, in hard but accurate movements. Professionals are usually very demanding of this little tool and choose it responsibly.

A good cuticle pusher is made of metal. It's shaped as a tiny trowel with soft rounded edges, about 1.5 to 2 millimeters thick, slightly wider than the nail base of your pinkie, repeating the shape of your nail and ending in a semicircle. Choose it with care: the wrong pusher can damage a nail or cuticle. When buying one, make sure it's nicely rounded without any angular bits and fits the nail following its shape. Use some rubbing alcohol or nail remover to disinfect it before use.

Of course you can find a cuticle pusher in most manicure kits. But buying a consumer-quality manicure kit is really not a good idea: you can discard most of the tools in it straight away before they ruin your nails. You're more likely to find the tools you need in specialized shops, professional supply stores, manufacturers' stores and manicure salons.

Prices may vary as much as $1 to $20, depending on whether the tool belongs to a respectable brand or some obscure label some of which are capable of producing tools of acceptable quality, too. You can even replace a cuticle pusher with your own nail, provided it has an oval tip, but naturally, you can only do it to yourself and never to another person.

Cuticle Softener

Formally speaking, it's not a tool but a whitish jelly-like substance in a pot. It looks a bit like nail polish and even has a brush inside. But we decided to include it with other tools because it performs a similar function: it prepares the cuticle for its easier removal and cleaning the nail.

Apply the substance onto and around the cuticle and wait for a couple of minutes: the hard, rough cuticle skin softens after which it can be safely pushed away or cut off. Before removing the skin, use a cotton wool pad to wipe any superfluous softener off the nail. By the way, soapy water has the same effect, only that it works slower and may dry out your skin. Also, a bottle of cuticle remover is so much easier to use on the go.

You can buy it pretty much everywhere, including manicure-supplies shops. But do make sure you buy the right thing: instead of cuticle softener, they may offer you cuticle dissolver. Although it serves the same purpose, it's a completely different formula aimed to destroy the cuticle, not to soften it. Cuticle dissolver lives up to its name as it gently removes the cuticle by dissolving its rough skin. Both cost around $3 to $8, and both require you to wash your hands thoroughly after use.

Cuticle Nippers

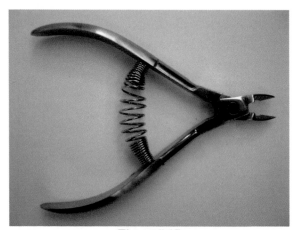

Figure # 17

Specially designed to trim the cuticle, they should be sharp as well as the right size for your nails. I'll use this opportunity to ask of you once again to take special care when choosing your tools. If you plan on removing your cuticles yourself, do not fall for poor quality multi-tool manicure kits containing so-called cuticle scissors that the manufacturer claims to be produced exactly for this purpose. Despite all the experience we have in this field, we're yet to come across a decent, let alone good, consumer-quality manicure kit. Chinese-made cuticle nippers won't do, either, because they're shaped differently.

Ideally, the length of the blades should be the same as that of your nails, 7 to 12 millimeters. For your own safety alone, you'd be better off shopping for nippers in a professional manicure supplies or manufacturer's store. We can't stress this strongly enough: in the past, we sometimes came across impressive-looking cuticle nippers produced by respectable cutlery manufacturers seeking to expand into a new market. They may use the right materials as well as know a thing or two about blades, but they are not familiar with manicure industry's specifications. They may have the right shape but it doesn't mean they have the right tool.

Figure # 18

Also, do not confuse cuticle nippers with pedicure clippers: they differ both in shape and in size. The best nippers are those with their handles connected by a length of spring (professional models will cost you $15 to $30).

Other Tools

For French manicure, you'll need guides. Stencils are good for airbrushing as well as for creating any clear, sharp designs. Nail art kits often contain ready-made guides and stencils; you can buy them separately or in sets, but you can also make them yourself using a strip of transparent Cellotape. When using Cellotape, it's crucial to make sure the surface you attach it to has completely dried out.

An Airbrush Gun is a tool to spray polish, ink or paint onto a nail. It's good both for drawing very fine lines and for color-filling. When used with a stencil, an airbrush gun allows you to create some very interesting gradual changes in color.

Nail Oil -- serves to moisturize and protect your nails.

Antiseptics -- as the name suggests, their purpose is to aseptisize and disinfect.

Chapter IV. Practice Section.
Eight Steps To Perfection

The second part of our book is entirely dedicated to practice. It contains nothing but examples -- we'll discuss the entire process of creating nail art, from the idea to its actual realization.

Keep in mind that you can use all the advice we give here in your everyday practice, as a foundation allowing you to create your own designs in the same vein. Just don't shy away from experimenting: we're prepared in advance to stake all our experience that nothing wrong can come out of it. Been there, done it.

We kept thinking why we wanted to call it an eight-step system. Why eight steps, why not seven, five or eleven? So we've spent some quality time analyzing all nail art operations. To our surprise, we've discovered there're exactly eight of them, no more and no less. We've merged all identical operations into respective steps and made those steps very clear and basic. Every step includes a detailed description of its purpose and exact procedure.

We've picked samples for this chapter making sure their choice allowed you to use as many various nail art materials as possible, so they don't necessarily differ in difficulty levels.

The Basics Of Composition

Composition in nail art deals with the design's cohesiveness, symmetry, and arrangement. From the very start, you should carefully consider your nails' shape. Take a close look at your hands: your nails are about to become tiny canvasses on which we'll be expressing our creativity.

The shape of your nails will determine how you break the background (not to mention if ever you decide not to divide it into color zones at all). When you don't use color to break the background into separate zones, you'll have to divide it up mentally, anyway. To do this, you need to draw one or two imaginary axis and build your composition around them. So that when you break your background into color zones, the borders between colors will also serve as composition axes. When your background is monochrome, you'll have to visualize your axes using your imagination.

To make it easier for you to visualize the whole thing, we include a chart showing different types of background-breaking designs depending on the nails' shape. Don't take them as gospel -- you might come up with your own ideas that work just as well -- but they're a good place to start.

These designs are based on one of two principles: they either repeat the nail tip's shape or are asymmetrical to it. This will allow you to use your axes to create either a symmetrical composition with two designs mirroring each other, or an asymmetrical one wherein the axes would divide the nail into two or several different zones. When creating an asymmetrical composition, don't forget that no matter how different the two halves of the nail are, they still need to create a visual balance.

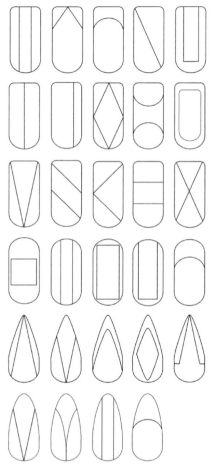

Figure # 19

Let's now discuss different axes positioning on the nails.

Type 1. A central vertical axis. This is the easiest design type. All you need to do is create a symmetrical or asymmetrical composition and paint it on your nails. Their shape will play the decisive role: if you choose an oval (Fig. C) or square (Fig. D) design, you'll be able to create a composition that's uniform all along its axis. If you create a composition for sharp (Fig. A) or almond-shaped (Fig. B) nails, you'll have to fill the nail base with more elements than its tip.

Type 2. A central horizontal axis. This can get slightly more complicated. The nail shapes as in Fig. C and D will still allow you to create a symmetrical composition, but in any case, you'll have to take into consideration the imaginary central vertical axis. And nail shapes as in Fig. A and B don't lend themselves easily to horizontal symmetrical composition. As for horizontal asymmetrical ones, they're extremely rare.

Type 3. A vertical axis cutting off one third of the design. This composition, too, is more suitable for shapes C and D.

Type 4. A horizontal axis cutting off one third of the design. Likewise, it's more suitable for C and D.

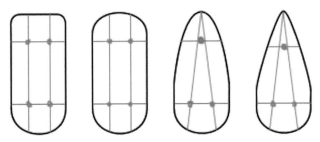

Figure # 20

For instance, you can use axes to create a net design: e.g., using two vertical and two horizontal ones. Their points of intersection can then serve as the composition's centers -- either symmetrical, or otherwise.

The composition itself is in fact a set of matching elements and empty spaces, arranged in balance around the axes and intersection points. Which matching elements are we talking about? It can be rhinestones (or little circles), ribbons (or stripes), foil shapes (like tiny stars and hearts), bullions (to lay into flower stems, petals or lines), etc. If you don't use any of the above, your composition may contain painted elements like dots, swirls and strips that you paint yourself using some water-soluble paints.

When putting a design together, you must consider empty spaces, as well. You need them so the design's composition doesn't becomet too busy, and so that the central element and the surrounding patterns are easy to see. Naturally, some designs don't use empty spaces at all, but their composition in this case is seemingly monotonous, as if the nail has been upholstered with a length of figured fabric.

When creating a composition, don't forget about balance. The entire nail has to be well-balanced against its central axis.

A few more tips:

- A large object is visually "heavier" than a small one;
- A dark object is "heavier" than a light-colored one;
- An object with a thick structure is "heavier" than one with a rare structure (e.g., a fine net is "heavier" than a large-meshed one, even if the thickness of the braid is the same);
- A bright color is "heavier" than a dull one. For example, if one corner of the design is occupied by a dark or bright small or thick element, the rest has to be filled with something light-colored and rare-spaced, even if it's an empty space or bare background;
- An empty space can have its own volume and "weight", provided it's big enough to accept it.

Finally, don't forget you aren't going to work with just one nail because you have five on one hand and five more, on the other. That's why, when working on a design, we need to keep in mind that it'll be multiplied by five -- or by ten, even, whenever your hands are close together. If you believe the design you're working on has gotten a bit busy, you can go one of two ways: you can either simplify the design or leave it the same on one nail (usually on your middle or ring finger), and use only small elements on it on the remaining nine.

If the design is very complex -- e.g., containing a feather or 3D nail art -- it is done on one nail only, and the rest are left plain without any designs at all.

Sometimes, a little thing like a dot or a line adds a finishing touch to a completed design. It's worth keeping in mind that the base and tip of the nail are not equal: our mind perceives the base of the nail as the beginning of an image, and the tip, as its end.

It's very possible you're not sure about many things at the moment. Just don't you worry, they'll all become clear as you start working. Practice makes perfect. Roll up your sleeves, and off we go!

Step One: Where You Get Your Ideas From

To borrow an existing idea and copy it is normal practice for a beginner. This route is also forgivable in a situation when you need to create a multitude of generic designs quickly -- for instance, when your salon is cracking under pressure and you don't have a minute's rest between appointments.

But if we're talking exclusive, if we talk limited edition, it's worth creating a new design from scratch. It's more fun, too. A designer job is one of a kind: it's light, refined and truly unique. Don't try to walk in somebody else's footsteps: do go your own way, do choose to be unique.

Have a good look around you: you might find nail art ideas everywhere if you're observant enough. Most unexpected objects can inspire a new design: a length of wallpaper, a fabric pattern, nature, insects' coloring, strange photos, building décor or even a candy wrap! Any of these elements can trigger or accelerate your creative processes resulting in your own authorial content.

Ready-made ornamental patterns work really well in nail art, by the way. Pick up a magazine and look through it for potential nail art elements: chances are, you'll find some. Even when it's not something you can use on your nails, try to work out what it is you like about it. It might be the picture's color or shape, its opalescence, a particular line or a ripple, or all of the above. Try to grasp and then define it in your miniature work of nail art.

You might need several sketches. If you feel you're failing to recreate the idea, you might need to study the original again to grasp its essence. If it sounds too complicated, try to start with simpler, easier to reproduce ornaments. Choose a plain element that doesn't contain any fine details because you won't be able to recreate them on a nail's tiny surface.

With time, you might develop a craving for image hunting that challenges you to create a beautiful nail design out of nothing: or rather, out of an evasive and almost non-existent image.

We would like to mention that, apart from the issues of professional methods and designer ideas, our examples also deal with positioning issues, each one addressing a particular nail art technique.

Figure # 21

Chinese Clouds

The author stumbled upon this idea when looking at hand massage balls. The little stylized cloud element served as a source of inspiration.

Figure # 22

Russian Emeralds

This one was ad libbed without any preliminary idea at all. The authors' desire to explore foil possibilities was too great to resist.

Figure # 23

Josephine

A swirl-based graphic ornament invokes the romantic atmosphere of days past, as does the net made of gold threads that might have been borrowed from a fairytale princess' garments.

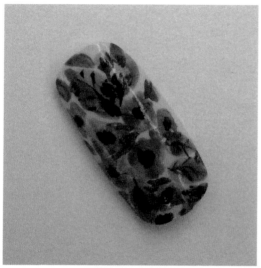

Figure # 24

Gardens Of Eden

An accidental purchase of a set of stickers inspired this one at the time: we liked the illusion of semi-transparency, similar to that of watercolor. In this case, we attempt to recreate the watercolor effect using acrylic. The design's soft purple lilacky flowers against the backdrop of mossy reddish leaves create an atmosphere of a charming, cosy summer evening.

Step Two: Arrangement And Composition

Before starting to actually work on the nails, it's always better to make a sketch of your future design on paper. Believe us we know what we're talking about. Sometimes we want to create something beautiful, something we can almost see in our imagination! But as soon as we start working, not really sure how the end result is going to turn out, our mental picture turns pale and dull, lines lose direction and... finally we reach for polish remover.

That's why you always need to make a sketch first. It's all right if the drawing's not very accurate, clumsy even, or if it contains errors and corrections. But you need to draft a sketch allowing you to grasp your design's idea.

It might not look too pretty at first, but you can always employ the assembly-line method. If you're serious about mastering nail art, try to draw a nail shape, enlarged three or four times, in your computer's graphics editor. Then multiply the image as many times as a page would hold, and print it out. Eh voila -- we've got blanks to fill with our creative ideas.

We're often asked which tool is best to use for sketching a design, with so many various types of paper, pencils, felt tip pens and even brushes available. The wisest thing to use would be something sharp and monochrome, like a pencil or a fine gel pen. It's easy to explain: fat lines will bleed and mix on your nails. Also, you can't use too many fine lines on a small surface like a fingernail: you'll need a magnifying glass to make them all out. So it stands to reason our future design can only contain details of average size.

This is a preliminary draft. To get a better idea of what you want, you can make a full-color sketch. It doesn't really matter which tools you use to paint it, as long as the drawing has some bearing on your mental image and give you an idea of what you can expect to see on your own nails.

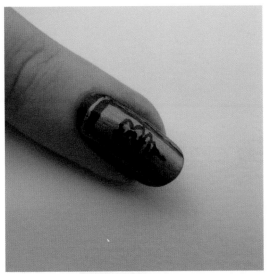

Figure # 25

Figure # 26

If we just paint the cloud element on top of the green background, it's not too interesting, really. To make the composition more pronounced, choose the tone of the background first, then place the little cloud in the middle and use a gold border to bring it into focus. It results in a centered, asymmetrical composition, which looks stylish and doesn't take much skill. The only requirement is a steady hand -- but even if it's not one of your fortes, it'll surely come with practice and time.

Figure # 27

Figure # 28

We've divided a sharp nail into several zones using background colors as borders. In the center, we've used some round rhinestones plus a diamond-shaped one, and some bullions lain out to form lines. The diamond is placed in the middle as the biggest element and composition's centerpiece. At the base, it's balanced with three smaller rhinestones that occupy a larger surface due to their number (a nail's surface is larger at its base), and by the tip, with only one (a nail's surface is the smallest by its tip).

To add finish, detail and celebratory look to the resulting composition, we lay bullion lines between the rhinestones, and use more bullions to line the borders between color zones which adds finish to our work. Here, it results in a centered, symmetrical composition.

Figure # 29

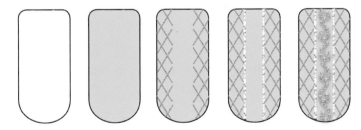

Figure # 30

We've used two silver strips to visually divide the nail into a central and two side zones. Please note the side zones are completely filled with a net covering them. Nevertheless, the net itself needs borders, it can't just end with nothing, it doesn't look nice, so we used our two silver strips to add a finishing touch. The middle strip contains a simple ornament that doesn't fill it completely, otherwise the nail would be too busy. Please note you do need empty spaces in your sketch.

Figure # 31

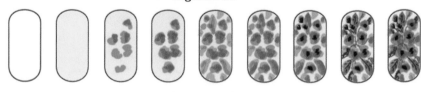

Figure # 32

For this one, we choose a neutral background first. The design covers the surface evenly, and the spots of color are uniform in their tone and strength all over the nail. Call it chaos in harmony, if you wish: every nail will sport a different flower-and-leaves arrangement but all the nails will still be kept in the same style. The only reservation is that the flowers should be placed more or less in the middle, with one or two little buds closer to the edges. The remaining space is then filled with leaves, large and small. It's important to create an impression of spontaneity so you don't need to overwork the fine details. Also, try to make sure you keep the arrangement well-balanced, so that flowers and leaves are equal in numbers and take more or less the same space.

Step Three: Practice

To master nail art, you don't need to die trying. But if we attempt to embrace the unembraceable, we'll discover our good intentions don't necessarily equal good skills. It takes practice to acquire a firm line, sharp eye and a steady hand, and it's best to do it while working on throw-away doodles you're going to use to discover and develop fine motor skills as well as your artistic taste.

You could practice on a fake nail or on a sheet of paper. If you don't feel very confident, just try to follow our instructions as you work. But as you perform the following exercises, please remember to recreate real-life conditions. For instance, when using a gel pen, you need to keep in mind that a real nail isn't as flat as a piece of paper and that the pen may and will be constantly sliding off it. Don't forget that a nail has a very small surface, so when sketching a future design on paper, you need to draw an outline of your nail first and continue drawing within its limits.

Example # 1: When working on this pattern, we suggest you use a fake nail to train your hand on first. Use a gel pen to draw the little cloud element as well as the straight lines. Don't press the pen too hard; don't strain your hand, either. A gel pen drawing can be easily removed from a fake nail with some water and cotton wool. Your own finger will do, too, although we don't recommend it: gel ink is a pain to wash off skin.

Example # 2: Practice laying bullions out onto the nail in neat lines. It takes some patience, but the result is worth the time. It's important that not a single little bullion breaks out of line.

Example # 3: Acquire the knack of meticulously drawing the swirly ornament with transparent glitter. To do that, you'll need a fine, short brush, a pot of transparent polish, and some glitter. Drop a small blob of polish onto some non-absorbant surface. With a brush, add some glitter to it and mix well. Pick up enough of the mix onto the brush to form a tiny droplet on its tip: this droplet we'll then use to place a dot in the center of our future swirl. Keep holding the brush at right angles to your fake nail or piece of paper while you drag the brush away from the dot's center to draw a little swirl. You might also wish to practice laying the net using lengths of silver thread.

Example # 4: Practice creating the watercolor effect. Even if you've never worked with acrylic paints before, now's a good time to get to know their qualities. Try mixing different colors and mark down the results you get. It's always better to use fake nails for training: unlike your own, they're disposable and won't need cleaning every time the attempt goes wrong. Also, practice painting fine lines and spots of color with a brush. Painting fine details with acrylics acquires a knack, but if you follow our advice, you won't find it hard to learn at all.

Step Four: Choosing The Right Tools And Materials

In the first chapter, we've discussed in detail the specifics of nail art tools and materials. Now let's be clear and tell you that not just any tools are a substitute for a hand-picked Tool Kit -- one with a big K. Every professional regardless of their qualifications must have a selection of their own personalized tools that fit their hand like a glove. They must be familiar with even the tiniest peculiarity of their use, and take these peculiarities into account when working on his or her own style in nail art. We admit that an individual selection like that could be put together over time and picked from various kits: average factory-assembled tools can rarely boast about their quality.

Example # 1: some mood-changing polish (the kind that changes its color depending on the light angle), thin transparent Cellotape, black polish, and two gel pens: black and gold. The Cellotape and black polish can be substituted with a fine brush and some black acrylic paint. Also: transparent polish, base coat, top coat and a primer kit.

Example # 2: transfer foil (or silver polish, or silver acrylic plus a fine brush, or good-quality silver glitter), pearly bullions, a few round small rhinestones and square middle-sized ones, mood-changing polish (or some metallic acrylic in moss) and a fine brush. Transparent polish, base coat, top coat and a primer kit.

Example # 3: transparent polish, cream-colored polish, silver glitter, self-adhesive silver foil strips (you can cut them yourself out of a kitchen foil roll), a length of silver thread. A pair of mini scissors, a fine short brush and a primer kit.

Example # 4: for this one, you'll need some transparent and cream-colored polish, as well as colored acrylics: raspberry, violet, blue, yellow, red, white, and black. The brush should be short and fine, preferably sable or a good-quality synthetic one. You need a brush with bristles that cling closely together with no individual hairs sticking out and come to a very fine point. Also, you'll need some water, a small water bowl, and a small white plate or a sheet of thick paper to use as a palette.

Step Five: Nail Preparation

Regardless of what manicure type you're about to create, you can prepare your pretty little nails using a few easy-to-follow rules. Keep in mind though that you shouldn't ignore them completely: they're time-tested and can be performed quickly in any circumstance.

First of all, you need to clean dirt from around your nails, and especially under them (if you have any to clean, that is). You can do it simply by washing your hands with some soap, after which you need to take a clean, soft paper towel and wipe its end hard under your nails. Just allow the soapy water to soften the skin under your nail properly first.

Secondly, we shape our nails:

- the square shape has well-defined, not rounded square corners with the nail's sides parallel to each other;
- the oval shape's rounded smile line mirrors the cuticle line;
- the almond shape doesn't have sharp corners; its smile line is rounded more than the cuticle line and has an even more rounded sharpish tip;
- the sharp shape has one sharp edge, that at its tip.

Having done that, we file off unnecessary nail surface (shaping it as desired), then use a fine file to smooth the edges. Brush your fingertip up and down the nail edge -- is it smooth enough now? Don't forget that besides its other benefits, filing helps to prevent your nail from splitting.

Thirdly, take a close look at cuticle skin. It's up to you whether you want to remove it or not. Basically, it's a rather complex bit of nail surgery -- sometimes dangerous, even, and is best left to professionals. These days, specialists practice a new type of manicure that leaves the cuticle intact, but it doesn't suit everyone. If you suffer from excessive cuticle growth or if it's damaged, it has to be removed.

One of the most common mistakes that lead to the poor condition of the cuticle is attempting to remove it incompetently on one's own. When it's removed entirely and frequently, it may lead to reddening and accelerate cuticle skin growth. It's a Catch 22 situation, in a way: the more often you cut away the cuticle, the faster your body attempts to grow it back. To stop the vicious circle, you need to stop cutting the cuticle yourself and seek professional help. If for some reason you can't contact a specialist, you need to apply special cuticle cream or oil, stop cutting it altogether, removing only hangnails if necessary, and limit yourself to pushing it back, provided it doesn't damage the nail bed.

To push cuticle skin away, you need to soften it first. There exist special products available for this purpose. You need to use one of several cuticle pusher types made of metal, rose wood or rubber. The procedure's simple:

- apply cuticle softener to skin around all five nails;
- once you've finished applying it to the fifth nail, return to the first one and use a cuticle pusher to push back the skin with gentle but firm movements;
- if the skin's too hard and won't move, apply more softener and wait a little;
- bear in mind that the correctly performed procedure shouldn't hurt at all;
- after the skin's been pushed back, remove the remaining softener from your fingers and wash your hands well.

Next, use some polish remover to remove any residual oil from your nails. Then, avoiding any contact of your nails with skin, apply a layer of transparent polish or a base coat.

Please note: if you use fake nails, you need to remove old polish from them first and if necessary, file to shape them as desired. Only after that a layer of transparent polish or base coat can be applied.

Chinese Clouds: suitable for the square or oval nail shape;
Russian Emeralds: suitable for the sharp shape;
Josephine: the oval shape;
Gardens of Eden: square or oval shape.

Step Six: Creating The Background

This is one of nail art's most fundamental issues. We'll do our best to describe the process in every possible detail, in the firm belief that in doing so we'll help eliminate a multitude of potential questions. Patience is the key word: if it doesn't go as well as you expected it to, take a break, have a think about what could have caused it, and... do it all over again.

Example # 1: The first layer is always either transparent polish or base coat. The second layer is green mood-changing polish. It's essential that it's perfectly dry and hard before you continue.

There're several routes available to create this particular background:

Firstly, we can do it using some black polish and Cellotape. Take a roll of transparent Cellotape and cut out an oblong rectangle with four straight, direct sides. You'll need three of them: one for your thumb nail, another for your index fingernail (as well as middle and ring fingernails), and one for your pinkie. Attach the Cellotape rectangle onto your nail making sure it sits tight and that its little corners aren't dogeared. It should leave stripes of uncovered surface on the sides and by the base of your nail; now we'll use black polish to paint over those uncovered bits. The black polish should be really thick so that one layer covers them completely. Once the black polish is dry, carefully remove the Cellotape.

Secondly, we can do it with some black acrylic paint (water soluble) and a fine shortish brush (0.01). We use them to carefully paint the imaginary stripes around our future rectangle. You might need to practice on fake nails or on paper first to make sure the stripes come out neatly and straight. Acrylics go onto paper similarly to regular paints, and form a film once dry. Once it's dry, it must be sealed with a layer of transparent polish.

Thirdly, we can use a stencil and an airbrush, provided you have one. Cover the nail with a Cellotape stencil the way you did

technique above. If the mix has gotten too thick, add more polish and glitter to it. Seal everything with a coat of transparent polish.

Example # 4: On a small plate, dilute acrylic paint with some water until it's rather weak and semi-transparent.

- Use your palette to mix green and mossy color spots: yellow plus blue will give you green, yellow plus tiny bits of black and blue will give you the moss color. Place a few green and mossy color spots onto the nail;
- Touch the leaves' tips with some light orange that slightly overlaps the green (yellow plus red will give you orange);
- A few blue and violet spots will serve as a base for the flowers, and light blue, for the buds (blue plus white will give you light blue).

Don't be put off by the slightly chaotic look, because later it'll be organized by retouching it with some thicker acrylic. Now we'll draw finer lines by using thicker paints. To do it properly, dunk the brush into well-mixed paint making sure there're no clots left on the brush, and then draw it along, barely touching the surface and holding the brush at the right angle to the nail, to paint thin stripes. In this manner we'll paint the leaves' veins and stems with dark green (yellow plus a tad of blue plus some black), the buds' shadows with blue, and the flowers' hearts with dark violet (violet plus black). Once dry, acrylic paints turn matt and rather dull. Cover the nail with two coats of transparent polish to bring brightness back into the acrylics.

Step Eight: Preserving The Finished Work

Now we've reached the final stage. If you've done everything right (and there we have little doubt) you should be pleased with the results: what you've got is a top quality nail art job your friends will envy and your boyfriend, admire. It goes without saying everybody will appreciate your newborn talent.

In the first case, our hard work resulted in a quite light and nice-looking design you can wear on a daily basis. The second example turned out rich and festive-looking. If you change the color scheme to, say, cream shades, you can offer it to a bride on her wedding day. The third example is the wedding type, but it can work well on a date, too, or just whenever you feel romantic. The fourth example looks fresh and will work well during the spring/summer season; it might suit creative and unconventional people. It will also look gorgeous on the beach.

But now it's time to discuss wear and tear. Unfortunately, no amount of certificates can give a nail art specialist the moral right to guarantee the longevity of their work. It'll last one or two days, for sure, provided its wearer doesn't go around playing war games or beating people up. Two weeks is an absolute maximum. But there're other factors involved that will decide on the longevity of your manicure.

Firstly, the duration of your nail art will depend on the materials you've used. A 2-D design will last longer, usually about a week.

Secondly, the nail preparation plays an important part. If you follow the preparation instructions listed in this book above, your nail art will serve longer. The key points here are making sure the nails are completely oil-free, as well as always using base and top coats.

Thirdly, individual peculiarities. With some people, polish starts chipping in less than twenty-four hours, which is their natural rejection processes at work, sad as it sounds. Some can wear polish for two weeks or even more.

Fourthly, your activity mode. You aren't likely to walk around with your hands in the air without touching anything. But it wouldn't be wise to go to the opposite extreme, either. Funnily enough, the myth that long nails and housework don't mix is nothing more than an urban legend. Indeed, it's rather true for fake nails, because if you "grow" a set of very long fake nails overnight, they will get in the way: you're not used to them and keep moving as if they're not there, so they keep catching and snagging on everything within reach. Naturally long nails don't give you these problems. But unfortunately, naturally long nails tend to be thin and fragile, which means you might need to use strengthening products.

Fifthly, every design has its own peculiarities. The weak point of the Russian Emeralds design is in the use of bullions. Their upper layer wears off very quickly, so we recommend you apply another top coat in twenty-four hours or so. But then you need to remember that an additional layer or polish may soften your nail artwork, so you need to be careful. Overall, the more top coats you apply -- within reason, of course, -- the stronger the manicure.

In any case, after some time your nail artwork will start to deteriorate. If you don't have much time or inspiration, you might try to renovate it by glueing back the missing rhinestones or refreshing the polish. Some designs can be remade into surprisingly new ones while others can't boast such properties.

It's worth remembering that the longest-lasting nail designs are those that involve nothing but polish. Good examples are marble patterns, as well as flat 2-D designs that don't have any protruding 3-D elements.

Example # 3: In the Josephine design, its glitter-and-transparent-polish-based pattern is very robust. The weakest points are the threads and bits of foil that can come unstuck. In this case, you need to glue them back into place with some transparent polish. If you can't do that, cut off the bits that stick out and cover the rest with more transparent polish.

Example # 4: The Gardens of Eden is a very stable design and may last for a rather long time. One thing to mention about using acrylics, though: as they're water soluble, any damage to the top coat will result in gradual destruction of the design every time you use water and soap. A simple rule you might need to remember, then: you need to retouch the damaged bit with transparent polish every time you've scratched, hit or rubbed off the artwork's upper layer. Same goes for filing or cutting your nails: the top coat creates a dome-like film over the acrylics and if its side gets cut or filed through, the acrylic beneath will be gradually washed out or will otherwise deteriorate.

Work Techniques

To complete our practice, we'd like to clue you in on the subject of the two most commonly used nail art techniques: classic manicure and French manicure.

Classic Manicure

It is important that the nails are completely dry and oil-free prior to polishing, to achieve good adherence and long-lasting results. To do that, wipe your nails with a wad of cotton wool soaked in polish remover liquid. Alternatively, you might file the nail with a buffer block intil the nail's surface becomes matt. If you've just removed the old polish, it stands to reason your nails are already oil-free. After oil removal, make sure your nail suface doesn't come into contact with the skin.

The method is as follows:

1. Always make sure you apply a base coat first. Ordinary transparent polish might do, too.

2. Take a pot of the color polish you're going to use and shake it gently a few times.

3. Dunk a brush into the polish and press it against the pot's neck in an upward motion to remove the excess of polish. You'll need more polish for your thumb (you might just dunk the brush into the polish, wait for a drop of excess polish to fall back into the pot and then paint the nail using first one side of the brush and then the other). Your pinkie will take very little polish. One dunk per nail: return your brush to the pot for each new coat.

4. Your brush shouldn't quite reach the nail's base. We touch the nail with the brush and then move the brush upwards all the way to the nail's base, then downwards to its tip in one straight stroke. We then repeat it to the right and to the left from the central stroke. You need to act quickly and carefully, and with time, you'll get the knack. Don't do it freestanding: it's best to place the manicured finger onto the table, as well as repose the wrist of your working hand on the table for better support.

5. While you apply the first coat to each of your ten fingernails, the first nail is already dry and ready for the second coat. The amount of coats depends on the polish itself, its color and texture, as well as quality. Normally, you'll need two to three coats. The first coat takes 10 to 15 seconds to dry out, the second, about two minutes, and the third, 5 to 10 minutes. The exact time depends on the particular polish. The thing to remember is to refrain from touching anything with your nails.

6. The polish is considered dry if two polished nails don't stick when they touch each other.

7. Any errors and smudges are then erased with the help of a correction pen.

8. Make sure you finish with a layer of top coat. It may have some extra properties, like matt or glossy wet look.

This three-layer formula (base coat, color, top coat) allows the manicure to stay on your nails for a week without chipping or cracking. No kidding! Such manicure will survive a decent amount of washing, cleaning and washing-up, regardless of what brand of color polish you use. It's worth mentioning though that if you use a base coat to level out imperfections, it might result in your manicure peeling off in one piece. That's why plain transparent polish makes the most reliable base and top coats.

It's worth mentioning that nail art follows the same set of rules as classic manicure, the only difference being that you apply a fancy design or jewelry instead of a plain color coat. When creating nail art, we should follow the three-layer formula as well.

French Manicure

Equally appropriate for a bride or business lady, it's good both for parties and for everyday life. It's acceptable for men, too. Its forte is in French manicure's ability to correct the nails' imperfections while preserving their natural look.

When doing it with nail polish, we either use a fine brush or a special guide. First, apply a coat of transparent or beige polish. Then cover the tip of the nail with white polish, not exceeding the nail's so-called smile line -- the line that serves as a border between the nail itself and its white tip.

It takes a bit of practice and a good quality brush to paint a steady line. It's much easier to trace the smile line using a guide. There are sets of nail guides available, ready for use. Basically, it's a strip of self-adhesive paper that you glue below the tip before polishing it. Once the polish is dry, remove the guide.

You can make French manicure guides yourself, too. Take a roll of ordinary transparent Cellotape, cut a strip 2 to 3 centimeters long and round one of its sides slightly with scissors to repeat the cuticle line. Ideally, the smile line should mirror the cuticle line.

French manicure follows the strict proportion of the tip's length being one-half of the nail base. There are special French manicure kits available, containing all necessary polishes and guides. The classic French manicure color combinations are beige, pink or nude for the base and white for the tip, but any pastel colors will do. It would be nice to finish it with a layer of transparent or transparent pink polish. It's also a great idea to use silver glitter for the tips.

Permanent French manicure is done with acrylic materials (not to be confused with acrylic paints). Any materials can be used for that purpose, and any extension technique would work. First, use a brush and special moulds to sculpt the acrylic ball of the required white consistency into the tip and fill the nail's base with some transparent mass slightly overlapping the white tip. A nail-extension professional can make the white tips with the help of a special pen.

In salons, there are special French manicure nail tips available that are glued onto your own. They don't demand constant correction and are suitable for those of us who are always pressed for time.

It's worth mentioning a new tendency in French manicure: highlighting, besides the white tips, the half-moon shape (also called a lunula) at the very base of the nail. Its line should be symmetrical to the smile line.

When creating permanent French manicure, it's important to make sure the acrylic material doesn't get onto the cuticle. For that purpose, you should always leave a hair-thin distance between the acrylic and cuticle. Filing also takes some care: if you overfile the tip or the lunula, the nail surface will differ in color.

Drawing With Water-Soluble Paints

One of the most interesting and challenging nail art techniques is creating artwork using water-based paints. To do that, we'll need a whole lot of various tools and materials, and we'll take time discussing each of them in particular.

Brushes can be made of squirrel, Kolinsky, or sable hair, as well as artificial fibers. Those made of Kolinsky or artificial bristles, in sizes 0, 00, 000, and 01, are especially good. Keep in mind though there are several systems of measuring the diameter of a paintbrush, so make sure you get the right size. In addition, we can use the following brushes:

- a dotting tool,
- a fan brush,
- a striper,
- a shading brush,
- a dagger brush,
- a round brush with a sharp tip for color-filling and applying glitter,
- a detailer medium,
- a detailer fine.

Liners are a special kind of polish with a fine brush inside. They're thinner than regular polish. But provided you have acrylic paints and some quality brushes, there's little point in also buying liners.

Gouache is a water-soluble paint containing water-based glue. For our work, we need to thin it down to the consistency of thick cream. Gouache's main disadvantage is in its bad adherence

properties: the paint doesn't stick to the nail's glossy surface. There're two ways of avoiding the problem:
1. File the nail surface with a buffer block to roughen it up. It's an effective solution but shouldn't be done too often as it doesn't do your nails any good at all.
2. Adding some PVA glue to your gouache paints, in a proportion of 1 to 4. It may sound scary, but in fact PVA glue makes a perfect addition to gouache paints, turning them into PVA-based tempera which has excellent adherence properties.

Acrylic paints (or water-soluble polymers) are in a league of their own. Thanks to their specific properties and the virtual absence of disadvantages, acrylics are the type of paints most suitable for nail art. Once dry, they create a water-resistant film and must be sealed with a layer or transparent polish or a top coat. Until you've done so, you can easily remove acrylic paint with water simply by rubbing the nail with a moistened wad of cotton wool. It's extremely convenient whenever the artwork or one of its elements has fallen below your expectations. As for old nail art, it's effaced with good old polish remover.

Speaking about techniques, if you want to cover an entire nail with acrylic paint, you need to wait until the paint dries out completely, and only then seal it with transparent polish. If later the nail plate is filed or broken, the damage to the seal will result in the paint washing away easily. Basically, acrylic paints offer themselves to unlimited 2-D creativity.

Color wise, acrylic paints come in regular (matt) and metallic. So basically, if you have a six or seven-color acrylic set (red, blue, yellow, white, black, violet and, optional, raspberry) plus metallic shades, nothing prevents you from completely forgoing polishes in your nail art arsenal, with the exception of transparent and specialist (heat-sensitive, fluorescent, etc) polishes.

Let's now discuss the optimum nail art solution: a set of acrylic paints and a few fine brushes. Not counting the preparation tools and materials, these are more than enough for effective nail artwork, and any craft shop carries them.

It's also a good idea to buy individual paints, not paint sets, because sets often contain inadequate or plainly useless colors. Unfortunately, non-specialists lacking arts background tend to have problems identifying colors correctly -- red being a good example. Shopping for a true violet is even worse: various manufacturers can tag a paint as violet while in fact meaning crimson (or raspberry) or ultramarine, while purple is situated between violet and red, and ultramarine, between violet and blue. Such near-misses are possible with virtually every color. For your convenience, here are the arts terms for the colors you need -- when shopping for paints, make sure you use their right names:

- ultramarine and/or blue;
- cadmium green;
- yellow medium;
- cadmium red deep, cadmium red medium;
- titanium white;
- carbon black;
- carmine (intense raspberry, purple)
- violet light

Figure # 33

It's better to buy fewer paints but of a better quality. Of the imported makes, we recommend Decolor and APA Color. The Russian-made Ladoga acrylic paints are inexpensive and of very good quality. You need to remember that good acrylic paints have to have the consistency of thick cream. If it's watery, stringy and/or lumpy, try to give it a good mix. If it hasn't made it creamy, try adding some water. But if it stays viscous, and/or if there are any residual lumps or flakes, just bin it. Keep an eye on the paints so they don't dry out: if necessary, add a small amount of water directly to the pot and mix well. Remember that once acrylic is dry, you can't thin it.

It's also a good idea to buy metallic acrylic paints in gold, gold light, silver, white silver, black silver, or bronze. Let your taste guide you into choosing the ones you prefer. One thing you need to keep in mind is that once diluted, metallic paints take on a nasty whitish tint. But once the paint dries out, it regains its magical gold or silver luster.

It might be worth buying acrylic paint tubes. Then you can squeeze some paint out onto a palette (a sheet of thick paper or a little white plate) and then transfer it onto a brush and mix the right color. Acrylics dry out in the open air very quickly. Also depending on how much water you've added to the solution, but normally, in ten minutes the paint's surface will be covered with a resinous film which is not water-soluble. It can also happen that bits of dry paint get onto your artwork resulting in an uneven surface.

Please remember that you should always mix colors on a palette, not on the nails themselves. Apart from the marbling technique when a few blobs of color are mixed into a swirling pattern, it's virtually impossible to mix colors well on the nail itself. And even with marbling, you need to make sure your acrylics are thin enough to prevent drying out until you're done.

Acrylics can be mixed in any combinations, so we suggest you try them out.

It's worth remembering there are only three primary colors, the rest are secondary. Black and white are either the complete absence of color, or the presence of all colors together at once. So let's now formulate the basic rules of color addition.

The primary colors are red (r), blue (b), and yellow (y).
Mixing equal quantities of each, we'll get:
b + y = green (g)
y + r = orange
r + b = in theory, that should result in violet, but on practice we get a nasty dirty burgundy color. So we complete our set by buying individual violet and raspberry paints. If we mix raspberry and blue (even better, ultramarine), violet is what we get.

You can make a color darker by adding some black to the paint.

You can make a paint lighter by adding some white, but remember that the resulting paler color will lose in brightness, too.

g + b = sea green

b + white = light blue

y + a tad of black = sap green

b + black + white = light gray blue (steel gray)

orange + white = cream

y + g + pistacchio

r + b + y = brown

Basically, using acrylic paints on a nail is identical to painting a miniature on paper.

Acrylics are best complemented by bullions, rhinestones, and glitters which add depth to your nail artwork. Still, be careful not to overdo it for too many might ruin the design's balance.

You need to practice holding the detailer brushes at a certain angle -- about 90 degrees -- when working on finer details. When you draw swirls, commas, and dots, you'll need a tiny droplet of paint on the very tip of your brush, which you then drag in the direction you need. If the design is picturesque and colorful, you might use light, transparent, overlapping strokes. You can use very thick paint, as well as very thin (don't forget to let it dry out properly so it doesn't smudge).

You can use very thin acrylics for a specific technique called paint-shaking. Place a blob of color, preferably contrasting the background, close to the base of your all five nails, then shake your hand vigorously a few times. The paint will leave thin veins of color which you can then decorate further with bullions or rhinestones.

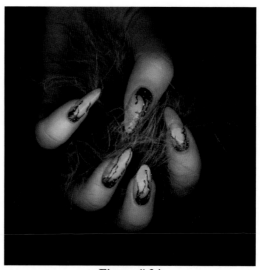
Figure # 34

In painting, there is a technique called feathering (or gradient fading), when colors blend with each other fading from one to the next. It's extremely difficult to recreate the fading effect with acrylics. To achieve a similar result, we need to mix all the intermediate colors on our palette. If you want your fade to cover the entire length of the nail, you'll need to mix three to five intermediate additional shades (that's not counting your main colors) and use them to cover the nail surface in stripes, gradually, one by one.

Figure # 35

Another thing to keep in mind is that using transparent polish to seal cream-colored acrylic may result in nasty yellow clots that ruin the entire work. To prevent this from happening, it's better to use cream-colored nail polishes instead. And if you use light-colored acrylics to cover the entire nail surface and then attempt to seal it with transparent polish, the whole thing might start to shrink and crackle. To avoid this, you need to either use nail polish for backgrounds, or alternatively finish the design first by drawing all the fine details over the acrylic background, and then seal the entire artwork with transparent polish. Mind though that in the latter case, had a design detail gone wrong, you wouldn't be able to erase it alone but would have to remove it together with part of the acrylic background which is indeed a pain.

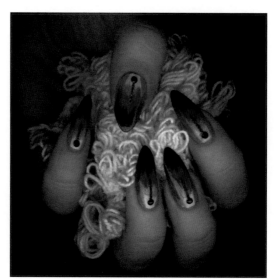

Figure # 36

Chapter VI. Some Useful Info About Your Nails

Today, we know so many ways to preserve youthful beauty. Wiping away wrinkles, getting a breast uplift, removing excess fat deposits -- everything's possible, provided you have the time and money. You may then look impeccable, but your hands will tell your real age to the attentive eye.

That's why we've decided to discuss a few things in this chapter we would normally consider trivial: the structure of our nails, their diseases and the basics of nail care. Wouldn't you agree that no amount of nail art can work wonders if the bearing material is no good?

The Nail's Structure

Just like hair, our nails are nothing but skin appendages, and their main function is protection. These plate-like horn growths are alive: they breathe, they have their own chemical activity, they exhale moisture, but looking after them doesn't involve offering them food or rest.

Hard nails serve as protection for tender fingertips whose objective is to feel the world around us. It might be worth mentioning that nails start to form and to grow at the moment of a person's birth. Before that, the foetus' nails do grow too, but unbelievably slowly.

A nail starts its growing inside the matrix -- a tissue which is in fact the heart of a nail. The matrix is a layer of cells that serves as a divider between skin cells and the nail plate. Hurting it can cause permanent damage to the nail and can even stop it from growing altogether.

A nail begins with a nail root, lying deep under the skin. The nail root is then channeled into the nail groove situated under the proximinal nail fold, right under the matrix.

Both the nail root and the matrix are protected by the proximinal nail fold in the very base of the nail. Above it lies a hard, white crescent-shape *lunula* which is in fact a continuation of the matrix. This is the area where the soft growing nail starts to harden and is especially vulnerable to damage.

The nail plate is a layer of dead keratin cells. Inside the matrix, compacted keratinocytes flatten and even out, thus turning into a nail plate.

The Nail's External Structure

The nail bed is a pink-colored area of skin stretching beyond the lunula. It abounds with capillaries that bring oxygen-rich blood to the nail bed, resulting in its healthy pink color. Physicians can tell the quality of blood circulation in a person's hand by simply pressing on a fingernail's bed.

The cuticle serves to fasten the nail plate to the proximinal nail fold in the nail's base which is called the hyponychium. It also hermetically seals the nail bed and the matrix from air and water. Without this protection, the temperature and humidity in this area would be too high to provide a baby nail's healthy growth.

The outer part of the nail is in fact the nail plate itself, restricted from three sides with the so-called nail folds: a proximal, or back one, and two side -- or lateral -- ones.

A nail fold is in fact a skin growth that creates a so-called nail wall when it meets the nail plate. *The nail walls* should be treated with special care during a manicure, for they house most of the unhealthy deposits both on the side of the nail plate and the nail fold. That's why insufficient sanitation of these areas (or, in plain English, not cleaning the nail's sides properly from whitish cuticle film, whether it's dry or rubbery) leads to the polish or acrylic peeling or chipping really quickly in these particular areas.

Nail plates thinner that 0.3-0.45 millimeters are a cause to speak about nail thinning; those thicker than 0.5-0.6 millimeters point to hyperkeratosis.

Nail Health

The color of your nails can tell a lot about your overall health and even help diagnose certain conditions: after all, the nail's horn-like substance (which is pure keratin) is being fed by our circulatory system.

A healthy person's nail is of evenly pink color. A yellow tint might signal the risk of liver problems, a red one, erythremia; people with congenital heart defects may have bluish violet nails. If your nails are covered in little white spots, you might have problems with central nervous system, while yellowish spots might point at certain problems with cerebral functions.

If you wish to have healthy, good-looking nails, the place to start is not nail care as such, but healthy, well-balanced nutrition. Your nails will only be healthy and strong if you receive enough of the vitamins, mineral salts and micro-elements listed below.

The effect of major mineral salts on the human body

Minerals	Sources
Sodium	Table salt and processed foods
Potassium	Fruit and veg, meat, cocoa. The best sources of potassium are potatoes, cabbage, cauliflower, apricots, peaches, pumpkin, and grapes.
Calcium	Milk and dairy products; dark green leafy vegetables
Phosphorus	Pulses, egg yolk, cabbage, fish
Magnesium	Pulses, cabbage, fish, bran
Iron	Spinach, nettles, liver, grapes, egg yolk
Zink	Grains, pulses, nuts, mushrooms, onions, liver, egg

	yolk
Cobalt	Beetroot

Also, you shouldn't forget that your body contains negligible quantities of certain chemical elements the absence of which make a whole lot of biological processes impossible.

The most important micro-elements in your body are iron, iodine, zinc, cobalt, fluorine, water, etc.

Vitamin B1 *(thiamin)*. Sources: yeast, bran, liver, cabbage, carrots, turnip, spinach, wheat sprouts, almonds, etc. It improves carbohydrate metabolism and central nervous system functions. Its recommended daily intake for adults is 2 to 5 mg.

Vitamin B2 *(riboflavin)*. Sources: brewer's yeast, cabbage, spinach, carrots, milk, egg yolk, fish, grains and pulses.

Its recommended daily intake for adults is 2 to 4 mg.

Vitamin PP *(Pellagra-preventive factor, B3, nicotine acid, niacin)*. Sources: pulses, fruit, veg, and animal products. Participates in the body's recovery and oxidation processes.

Its recommended daily intake for adults is 15 to 20 mg.

Vitamin B6 *(piridoxin)*. Sources: bran, liver, kidneys, brewer's yeast, grains, peas, etc. Bananas are especially rich in this particular vitamin.

B6 deficiency manifests in muscle weakness, anemia, and fatty liver disease.

Vitamin B12. Sources: animal products. Participates in protein and carbohydrate metabolism.

Its absence leads to anemia caused by carcinoid formations.

Vitamin C *(Ascorbic acid)*. Widely common in all fruit and veg, especially rose hips, all citrus fruit, red peppers, sorrel, potatoes, parsley, etc.

Its recommended daily intake is 70 to 120 mg.

Lack of this vitamin leads to fatigue, low immunity, nasal and dental bleeding. Its complete absence results in scurvy.

Vitamin B15 *(Pangamic acid).* Widely common in nature. Participates in metabolic processes.

Vitamin P1 *(Rutin).* Sources: all fruit and veg, especially the rind of citrus fruit, black currant, rose hips, cowberry, tea, etc.

Its recommended daily intake is 50 mg.

Vitamin A *(Retinol).* Sources: animal products. Provitamin A is found in vegetable products. The biggest sources of Vitamin A are liver, codliver oil, egg yolk, and dairy.

Provitamin A *(Beta-carotene).* Found in dark-green fruit and vegetables (spinach, cowberry, etc) and dark-yellow and red fruit and vegs (carrots, tomatoes, red peppers, etc.)

The recommended daily intake for Vitamin A is 1.5 mg.

Vitamin D *(Calciferol).* Sources: Codliver oil, egg yolk, butter, caviar.

Its recommended daily intake is 500 to 1000 mg.

Vitamin E *(Tocopherol).* Sources: vegetable fats (especially corn oil), green beans, green peas, lettuce, wheat, corn, etc.

It regulates reproductive functions and improves endocrine system and metabolism. Its presence improves absorbency of Vitamin A.

Nails And Their Problems

Brittle, Fragile Nails. To strengthen your nails, try nail baths of warm Vitamin A-enriched vegetable oil with the addition of three drops of iodine or five drops of lemon juice, one or two times a week.

Also, seawater baths are great for strengthening brittle nails. If you can't afford going to the seaside three or four times a year, buy some sea salt and use it to have daily 10-minute nail bath sessions for a whole month, several times a year. The salt dosage is usually marked on the bag. Alternatively, you can make a nail bath using ordinary kitchen salt (1 tablespoonful for a cup of water) with the addition of one drop of iodine.

Another excellent nail strengthening idea is rubbing in some lemon, cranberry or currant (black or red) juice.

Very effective for nail strengthening is bee's wax. Melt it gently over some warm (not boiling) water and place your fingers into the wax. Keep the resulting beeswax "thimbles" overnight.

Flaking Nails. This problem can be caused by fungal infections, but also by handling certain chemicals and solvents. Always wear safety gloves while using them and make sure you apply a protective coat over your nails. Another reason for flaking may be a bad-quality file (e.g., a diamond one).

If Your Nails Started Yellowing. If you're sure the yellowing is not caused by a medical condition, you might try to bleach your nails with 3% hydrogen peroxide or with some lemon juice. You can also make a special nail whitening mix:

One part glycerin, 5 parts hydrogen peroxide.

Or: 1 part glycerin, 1.5 parts peroxide and 4 parts distilled water.

Hangnails. Don't attempt to bite or tear them off. Instead, remove them with a special formula or a pair of clippers and don't forget to rub hand cream into your fingers regularly!

Only if it's constant and persistent, nail care can improve your nails' appearance.

Nail Care

Any woman will tell you that nails are one of the most vulnerable body parts. They're usually left exposed, facing the elements like open air, wind and sunrays. Washing up should also be done occasionally, and hot water combined with washing-up liquids and cleaning stuffs make nails thin and brittle.

The easiest way to restore one's nails is a lemon mask. Place a thick slice of lemon onto a plate and dig your nails into it for a good 50 to 70 seconds. You might find it strange, but they'll turn white and shiny. Please mind though that this mask isn't advised for very dry and brittle nails.

A seawater bath is another nail strengthening solution. Add two tablespoonfuls of bath sea salts to a cup of warm water and submerge your nails in it for 15 minutes. Adding a few drops of lemon juice to the bath will have an additional whitening effect on your nails. You can also add some essential oils like ilang ilang or lemon (adding a few drops of the oil to the salts before mixing them with water will facilitate its dissolvability). Do it daily for two weeks, followed by once or twice every week.

Another, less exotic, nail strengthening solution is applying a warm mixture of vegetable oil and plain kitchen salt. Not brain surgery, is it?

Having sea salt nail baths once a week is a good idea, dipping them into warm olive oil is an even better one. You can also buy special cuticle oil. Try to find some time -- on weekends at least -- and treat your nails to a moisturizing mask: rub some moisturizing cream into the skin around your nails, put on a pair of Latex gloves and keep your hands warm by covering them with a towel for about 10 minutes, then remove the excess cream with a paper towel.

Herbal baths with thyme or St John's wort will help strengthen your nails, too. An infusion of St John's wort will help improve your nails' health while thyme will soften the skin around them, helping to fight hangnails, too.

Just remember that nails are brittle for a reason -- or rather, several. Inadequate nutrition causing calcium and vitamin deficiency, the drying effects of cleaning and washing-up materials, and using scissors for cutting your nails (which causes nail deformities) are only a few.

You should use a file to shape your nails. Filing should be done in smooth motions from the sides to the middle of the nail. Don't dig too deeply into the sides which might trigger ingrown nails. Nails shouldn't be too short: they must extend beyond the fingertips. Long nails should be cleaned from the inside daily with a brush and soap or with a cotton bud soaked in lemon juice.

Indiscriminate, we tend to use metal files, choosing sharper ones then filing the poor nail off in each and every direction.And that's exactly the type of file to cause the most flaking damage. To avoid it, choose a ceramic file or newer triple-cut metal files.

Don't forget the base coat, either: it contains matrix-nurturing oils and vitamins strengthening the nail's base and root and thus improving its growth. Also, the base coat prevents aggressive environments such as nail polish from thinning out and destroying the nail plate. Base coat also prevents polish from coloring the nail. It's also important to choose base coat correctly: ideally, you should seek a specialist's advice, but in any case try to make sure your base coat, main polish and top coat are of the same make.

It's also not a good idea to wear polish all the time: nails need some rest, too. By the way, the nail "breathes" with its matrix, under the cuticle. That's why it's important to leave some unpainted space down by the latter. Overall, the matrix is extremely sensitive, its cells dying from the slightest impact causing the nail to darken, crack or even peel off.

If you've broken a nail, don't rush to pare the other ones to the same size. If you're desperate enough, the nail can be fixed in any modern-day salon by glueing or extending it. If one of your nails is cracked, you can have it patched with some natural silk.

But you don't need to head for a salon to patch up unhealthy nails. First of all, say no to polish for the time being and limit yourself to applying calcium-rich base coat daily. After three or four days, remove the base coats with some polish remover and start it all over again. Another good thing is to use a keratin-based nail treatment rich in vitamins: today, every specialist nail care brand has its own. We're talking about liquids here, not pills -- the thing to do is make sure the treatment gets under the lunula at the nail's base.

A Few More Words About Polish:
- have a look at your sweet little nails. Light-colored polish -- better matt than pearly -- will conceal unevennesses and furrows. Wide nails will profit from darker colors;
- always use a base coat: the polish will last longer, and the nails won't turn yellow;
- never apply nail polish after a bath or shower: the heat and steam will have caused the nails to expand resulting in poor adherence of the polish;
- to ensure polish doesn't get onto the skin around the nail, always apply it starting from the middle of the nail;
- little errors are easy to remove with polish corrector pens;
- to prolong the nails' shine, cover them with an extra top coat.

Hand Care

Your hands with their little nails are constantly busy, whether it's doing housework or jesticulating to help an excited conversation along. Hand skin has virtually no reserves of fat and moisture of its own, and constant contact with cleaning stuffs in combination with frequent hand washing aggravates the situation even more. It results in wrinkles, roughness and cracks.

But it can be avoided if only you follow a few simple steps. For one, always wipe your hands dry after washing them. Try not to use electric hand dryers, and don't forget to apply hand cream regularly.

If your hands are seriously damaged, you might need to apply a much thicker layer of cream, put on a pair of cotton gloves and leave the cream on overnight. When choosing a hand cream, read the packaging for its degree of sun protection. The higher it is, the better protection it offers against wrinkles and pigment spots.

Plan a half-hour manicure session once a week every week. Purchase a quality nail file (ceramic ones are the best) and an orange stick to push away the cuticle. It's not a good idea to cut it off on your own as it'll only grow faster and thicker every time. It can be removed with special lotions which also slow down its regrowth. For smooth and shiny nails, polish them with a special cushion.

There is, of course, lots of other hand care advice. Here's some of it:

- pay attention to how you wash your hands. It's advisable to use soft water for this simple hygiene procedure; you can soften hard water by adding a tablespoonful of bicarbonate of soda for a liter of water;
- always wash your hands with warm water: cold water will cause hand skin to flake, and hot water will lead to limpness;
- use liquid soap (or handwashing gel or foam) that contain moisturizing and softening agents; you can also use baby soap because it's specially developed for sensitive skin;
- for flaky hands, make a mixture of lemon juice, linseed oil, egg yolk and honey and apply before going to bed;
- you can always make a hand mask: cook some oatmeal, mix with a little vegetable oil and apply to your hands for 10 to 15 minutes before going to bed;
- for soft skin and to prevent flakiness, make an oatmeal hand bath: cook some oats in plenty of water, drain and place your hands in the liquid for 10 to 15 minutes;

- mashed potatoes are very tasty, but they also make an excellent hand wrap: cover your hands with warm mashed potatoes, then wrap your hands in cellophane and cover with a bath towel to keep them warm for 15 to 20 minutes;
- if you've been doing some hand washing, rinse your hands in a weak vinegar solution. Alternatively, apply some lemon juice, or yoghurt, or sour milk;
- for soft and supple skin, you can smother your hands in a mixture of equal quantities of olive oil and kombucha tea, especially overnight: in this case, you'll need to wear a pair of cotton gloves in order not to stain your bedclothes;
- to get rid of redness, you might use contrast hand baths: submerge your hands into bowlfuls of cold and hot water 10 to 15 times, finishing with cold water, then massage your hands with some vitamin-rich nourishing cream before going to bed;
- as an alternative, add a few drops of milk or cream to the water you wash your hands in to gradually get rid of the redness;
- as yet another alternative, sea salt hand baths seem to really work for red hands. Mix 200 grams of sea salt into a liter of water, boil it for a short while then cool down a little. Place your hands in the resulting health-spa "sea water" for 15 seconds, followed by 5 seconds in cold water; repeat several times and finish with smothering your hands in a rich hand cream.

Also, don't forget a few simple rules to protect your hands from environmental hazards. Follow these simple recommendations for smooth, supple, beautiful hands:

- before going out, apply a generous layer of protection or nourishing cream, then wipe away any extra with a paper towel. Moisturising creams are good, too: they absorb quickly and don't leave oily traces;

- hand cream should be applied to your hands and elbows twice a day, mornings and evenings. You can also rub some rich cream or oil into your skin and nails;
- if it's windy or chilly outside, it's a good idea to wear gloves;
- at home, you'll need gloves, too: the household rubber type for washing, washing-up and other "wet" activities, and cotton gloves for "dry" household cleaning duties. They'll protect your hands from dirt and aggressive cleaning agents.

Nail Extension

It's common knowledge that untidy hair and unkempt hands ruin a woman's looks. The thing is, knowing how to look after one's appearance is not enough: leading a healthy lifestyle is just as important. But if you need results fast, you might consider building the missing nails up. So here we're going to reveal a few extension secrets.

Counterindications

We can't deny that nail extensions made with artificial materials like acrylic or gel can indeed lift or become unstuck. No need to close our eyes to this problem. Sometimes, you'd have your nail extensions done and are very happy with the technician's job. But literally the next day (or the day after) virtually all your nails start to fall off!

What's that, you might ask. The technician not doing her job properly? Low quality materials? If these are the case, then nail extensions done by another technician or with different materials will last longer. You might want to try having your extensions done by another technician or with different materials. But if the nails start to lift again, you yourself are the cause. It happens, unfortunately, because not every human body is happy to accept foreign bodies. Sometimes, they trigger rejection processes. Here're the reasons for your body trying to get rid of nail extensions:

- artificial materials like acrylic or gel are wary of cold, moist hands: they're the symptom of heightened perspiration. The nails won't stay put because it's impossible to degrease the nail plate. As a rule, it applies to very thin nails;
- if you've just finished a course of antibiotics, your body has started elimination processes which work through your hair, nails and skin. Trying to get rid of the antibiotics, your body rejects everything else it considers unnecessary;
- if you're taking a course of hormone treatment, it's affecting your acetone balance. The increased amounts of acetone in your body will cause artificial materials like acrylic or gel to lift. The same scenario is true for women with inadequate hormonal background.
- if you're pregnant, your hormonal system is being rebuilt completely and your body is guarding itself against everything that's not necessary. Which leaves you no chance to sport nail extensions during pregnancy.

So we suggest you think of all of the above before deciding on nail extensions. If you've had them before and they wouldn't stay on -- have mercy on yourself and the technician and reconsider. Both nail extension materials and the extension technique remain the same: there haven't been any recent magic-bullet breakthroughs in this area.

Nail Extension Techniques

As with any process requiring time, decision and devotion, the nail extension has its own techniques and peculiarities. As for techniques, there're three of them, and we'll speak of each one in particular and discuss their pros and cons. One thing we'd like to mention from the start is to forewarn you against overdoing it:

extensions add extra weight to your nails so it's not a good idea to go too far, for fear of ending up, instead of elegant feminine nails, with a set of claws à la Freddy Krueger.

Fabric Wrap Technique

If you have healthy, well-shaped nails (which we sincerely hope you do) and you just want to make them longer (maybe because you're fed up with waiting for them to grow, or because you break them often, whatever), this is the right technique for you. The name speaks for itself: fabric extensions are used on top of fake tips. Virtually every nail art salon is capable of providing it (and we strongly disadvise experimenting on yourself in the comfort of your own home):

- your nails will be filed down and tips attached, then shaped with a special pair of clippers (let not tools' names scare you: all the tools are miniscule and can't do any harm in the hands of an experienced professional) and scissors;
- pieces of fabric (like silk or linen) will then be cut out to fit your nails' shape and glued on top of your own;
- you're done, time to polish it!

Pros: fabrics virtually don't irritate skin around the nails and the nail itself suffers little. Also, this method is good for fixing broken or cracked nails.
Cons: fabric nails are short-lived and break easily. Today, this technique is mainly used as an additional reinforcing measure, and also for fixing broken nails.

Gel And Acrylics

Another scenario: you're so unhappy with your nails (their shape, length or uneven surface) you've decided to completely reshape them. In this case, first they'll file your nails down almost to the quick, leaving only a couple of millimeters, then polish them with a soft file to make the surface as smooth as possible, finishing off with a special nail oil remover. After that, you're strictly forbidden to touch your nails (or all that oil removing would have been for nothing). The technician will then insert a special little plate under the remaining two millimeters of your nail. This plate is the form used to shape your new artificial nail, made of gel or acrylic.

First, let's speak about the **gel technique**. Gel nail extensions can be built using both fake tips and forms:
- using a brush, apply gel (a sticky, gluey substance) to the nail;
- Put the nail under a UV lamp for 2 to 3 minutes until the nail is set;
- you might need 1 to 3 coats of gel, depending how hard and strong you want the nail to be;
- shape the nail to the desired length.

The whole thing from start to finish will take 2 to 3 hours. It's worth mentioning that gel extensions are considered safe but take a bit of getting used to. Gel cracks easily under pressure and repeated visits to the technician are likely. We also suggest you make sure that the technician uses a special resin, harmless for the body. You should choose your nail technician with the same care as you do your hairdresser: both have their unique place in your life.

Pros: gel nails look very nice, they're usually shiny and transparent, so there's little need to paint them at all. And the UV rays used for hardening the gel also help prevent fungal infections.

Cons: a gel extension is not at all easy to get rid of: it'll have to be sawn off which is an unpleasant procedure that does your nails little good. Also, if one of the gel nails cracks or breaks, it can't be fixed: a broken nail will have to be cut off.

Now let's speak about **the acrylic technique**. Nail technicians borrowed both the method and the materials for it from dentistry already twenty years ago. In this case, we're talking about acrylic powder which, once mixed with a special acrylic liquid, turns into a thick viscous substance that hardens quickly once exposed to the air, just like a tooth filling in the making.

This method demands considerable experience from the technician using it, as well as a certain amount of talent:

- the new acrylic nail has to be sculpted with the most miniscule of tools which requires the skills of both a sculptor and a jeweler; it has also to be done as fast as possible before the mixture hardens;

- then the nail has to be filed to the desired shape, polished down and covered with a special powder -- pink, white or any other color of your choice -- after which it's considered done.

This extension procedure takes two to three hours. But you need to know in advance what it might cost you. Keep in mind that acrylic can eat through the nails' keratin layer leading to their damage (but it can't ruin your nails for good as some say, this is just an urban legend), and may also increase the risk of fungal infections.

Pros: Acrylic nails are the strongest, and you need to go some to break them. If you do manage that, you can have your broken nail fixed in the salon (which will cost you 50-70% of the original extension price). Acrylic nails are almost as supple as natural ones. They're easy to remove, too: acrylic can be dissolved in special liquid for the same 50-70% of the original extensions price.

Cons: Acrylic has a strong specific odor, although it tends to weaken and disappear over time. While odorless acrylic exists, he doesn't adhere to nails as well. After removing polish, you might find out that the acrylic nail has lost its shine -- and if you've used acetone-based polish remover, the acrylic will have turned yellow. So you'll be obliged to cover it with polish once again.

Maintaining Nail Extensions

You need to keep in mind that once extensions are done, your nails will require special care. At first you'll have to relearn how to do many everyday operations using your new extended nails: buttoning shirts, pressing computer keys, etc etc.

Normally, after about two or three weeks of wearing extended nails, you'll need to have them retouched for about half the full extension works price. A technician will retouch the border between your own and fake nail; she will file it down to a desired length, reduce its thickness in half by buffering and finish it off the same way as the first time. Wearing a fake tip demands having its length modified and a new layer of gel applied.

You can paint a fake nail with regular polish; for its removal, non-acetone polish removers are recommended. Polish lasts well on fake nails because they don't produce any oil that contributes to polish peeling. If necessary, they can be buffered and filed using very fine files.

If expertly done, artificial nail extensions and their consequent retouching and removal don't harm nails at all. Still, for about a month after removing gel or acrylic tips, your nails will hurt quite a bit while looking miserably thin. But with competent care, they will soon be restored back to their original qualities and may even start growing faster than before you had the extensions done. More than that, if you used to have unseemly, spade-shaped nails, they'll now grow nice and smooth, much to their happy owner's joy, as they've learned to grow straight in their close contact with the ideally shaped "prostheses".

Finally, a word of warning. Do not attempt to opt out on the nail extension precedure by fitting yourself with fake plastic nails abundant in every dollar store. Thick fakes will have a negative effect on weakened nails, and the cheap chemical glue that comes with every pack contains some very unhealthy ingredients! Also, the only way to remove them is by peeling them off the nails while nail extensions are carefully filed down by a professional.

Post-Extensions Nail Care

It's not a secret you shouldn't wear nail extensions all the time: we'd advise you to remove extensions after every 6 to 8 months to offer your nails the chance to have some proper rest.

After the extensions' removal, we'd recommend you treat your nails to some vitamin treatment or other. This will help restore and prime them for the next extension session as soon as possible. Offer your nails a regular healing bath. You can make them yourself with some olive oil and a few drops of lemon juice to keep your fingers in for 15 minutes or so. For strong and healthy nails, try rubbing in some dill or parsley leaves. If your nails are fragile with white spots, try rubbing lemon juice in the skin around your them, and vitamins A,E and D into the nail plate itself.

Vegetable oil-based nail bath: Take equal parts of castor and sunflower (or olive) oil and add a few drops of 2 to 5% tincture of iodine.

Herbal nail baths: These are the herbs we recommend: valerian, chamomile plant, heartsease and dill. Brew one part herbs in three parts boiled water and leave for some time, then place your fingertips in the resulting infusion for 10 to 15 minutes. Do it every other day for a month and finish with rubbing some cream into the skin around your nails. This treatment is good not only for post-extension nails having a break, but also to improve the natural nails' strength and nutritional balance.

Specialist Glossary

When talking to us, our friends -- and sometimes even nail art professionals -- tend to use "specialist speak" we don't understand a word of. They use professional manicure and nail art terms that help define and understand their technicalities. So we've compiled a small glossary of the more common words and expressions. Don't attempt to remember everything at once: it will come naturally with practice if you keep referring to it.

A

Acupressure -- type of reflexotherapy that uses finger pressure on the acupuncture points

Acupuncture -- type of reflexology that involves sticking special needles into the acupuncture points

Alaminol -- a disinfecting solution

Albinism -- a disorder characterized by absence of skin, hair and iris pigmentation

Alpha axyacid complex -- a complex of natural acids (glycolic, citric, malic, tartaric, lactic) for a chemical peel

Anolite -- a disinfecting solution

Anonychia -- absense or atrophy of nail plates

B

Bacteria (pl; sing., bacterium) -- a large group of mono-cell organisms

Basal layer -- the epidermal layer responsible for cell multiplication

Beau's lines -- deep grooved lines that run from one side of the nail to the other

Body piercing -- the practice of making holes through the skin to hold various jewelry

Buff -- a type of nail file

C

Callous -- a thick build-up area of the skin's upper layer

Chloasma -- blotchy, brownish skin pigmentation

Chloramine -- a disinfectant solution

Collagen -- a protein found in connective tissue

Cuticle -- part of the proximal fold covering the growing part of the nail

D

Dehydrating substances -- those used to temporarily dehydrate the nail's surface

Derma -- the deep inner layer of the skin

Dermatitis -- inflammation of the skin

Diplococcus (pl. diplococci) -- a patogenic bacterium causing various infections

Disinfection -- measures to remove the causes of infectious diseases

Dyschromia -- a disorder characterized by changes in nail pigmentation

E

Eczema -- a chronic inflammatory skin disease

Epidermis -- the outer layer of skin

Eponychium -- the thickened layer of proximal fold adjucent to the nail

Erysipelas -- an acute bacterial infection of skin and mucous membranes

F

Fabric coating -- silk, fiberglass, linen

Folliculitis -- purulent inflammation of hair follicles

Formaldehyde -- a colorless biodegradable gas with a strong odor, product of animal and vegetable bioactivity

Formalin -- a 40% solution of formaldehyde

Freckle -- a small pigment spot on the skin

Furuncle (boil) -- an acute inflammation of hair follicles

G

Glycerin -- thick transparent oily liquid used in medicine

Grain -- a nail file's degree of abrasiveness

Granular layer -- another epidermal layer

H

Hair -- a skin appendage

Hapalonychia -- abnormal nail softness

Hippocratic nails -- clubbing of nails, drumstick fingers

Horny layer -- the outermost layer of the epidermis

I

Ingredients -- parts of a certain substance

K

Keratin -- fibrous proteins found in hair, nails and other horn-like substances

Koilonychia ("spoon nails") -- a disease causing the nail plate to flatten and concave

L

Lanolin -- an animal wax-like substance with softening qualities

Length of the nail -- the distance from the smile line to the nail's free edge

Leukonychia -- nails' discoloration resulting in whitish spots

Look, a -- a person's style

Lunula -- the visible bit of a nail's growing part, especially pronounced on the thumb and index finger

M

Maceration -- using water-based solutions for cuticle softening

Manicure -- cosmetic care of the hands and fingernails

Manicure, cuticle nipping -- a type of manicure that involves cutting back the cuticle with a pair of cuticle nippers

Manicure, dry -- a type of manicure that uses special chemical substances to soften the cuticle

Manicure, European -- a type of manicure that involves grooming the cuticle without cutting it back

Manicure, French -- a bicolor manicure using two shades of polish

Manicure, hot -- a type of manicure that uses special substances at hot temperatures to soften the cuticle

Manicure, wet -- a type of manicure that uses water baths to soften the cuticle

Massage -- a healing system of applying mechanical force to a person's body

Matrix -- the growing part of the nail

Melanin -- a pigment substance of human skin

Microbe -- a tiny one-cell organism unseen to a naked eye

Micronychia -- abnormal smallness of the nails

Moisturizers -- substances that lock the skin's own water

Mycosis -- a skin disease caused by various types of fungi

N

Nail -- an appendage of skin

Nail bed -- a part of the nail serving as a base for the nail plate

Nail extension -- a procedure of strengthening and lengthening one's nails with the help of articifial materials

Neurodermatitis -- a genetic skin disorder accompanied by strong itching

O

Onychauxis -- a disorder resulting in the abnormal thickness of the nail bed layer

Onychoblastus -- the horn-like substance of the human body

Onychodystrophy -- a disorder affecting a nail's shape, size and condition

Onychogryphosis -- abnormal claw-like curving of the nails

Onycholysis -- loosening of the nail from the nail bed

Onychomycosis -- a fungal disease affecting the nails

Onychorrhexis -- a vertical split of a nail

Onychoschisis -- a horizontal split of a nail

P

Paraffin therapy -- a medical treatment that involves applying warm paraffin to parts of the body

Paronychia -- an infection of the nail folds

Pedicure -- cosmetic care of the feet and toenails

Peel -- a cosmetic treatment aimed at removing the rough upper layer of skin

Prickle-cell layer -- one of the layers of epidermis

Professional ethics -- the rules every salon adheres to

Proximal fold -- the fold of skin around the nail making the nail fold

Psoriasis -- a genetic disorder affecting human skin, joints, kidneys and liver

Pterygium, I -- a film-like transparent strip of skin under the cuticle

Pterygium, II -- a condition resulting in an overgrowth of pterygium and/or cuticle

Q

Quality certificate -- a document confirming the product's compliance with required industry standards

R

Reticular region -- the layer of skin containing venous and arterial blood vessels

S

Scabies -- contageous skin disease caused by skin mites

Sebaceous glands -- skin glands producing skin oil

Smoothing products -- softening and soothing substances

Solvent -- an ingredient responsible for the thickness of nail polish

Staphylococcus -- a type of pathogenic bacteria causing a wide range of diseases

Sterilization -- the process of complete destruction of microorganisms

Sterilizer -- a machine for sterilization

Streptococcus -- a type of pathogenic bacteria causing a wide range of diseases

Sudoriferous glands -- the skin glands secreting sweat

T

The skin's mantle -- a protective layer of acid fats on the skin, created by the products of its metabolism

Toluol -- a type of solvent

V

Vaseline -- a softening, soothing, moisturizing product

Virus -- a microorganism causing infectious diseases

Vitiligo -- discolored pale patches of skin

1050167R0

Printed in Great Britain by
Amazon.co.uk, Ltd.,
Marston Gate.